The Little
Capoeira Book

Other books by Nestor Capoeira

Capoeira: Roots of the Dance-Fight-Game. Berkeley,
California: North Atlantic Books, 2002.

In Brazil

Capoeira, o pequeno manual do jogador. São Paulo: Ground,
1981. Fourth edition, revised. Rio: Record, 1998.

Capoeira, galo já cantou. Rio: ArteHoje, 1985. Second
edition, revised and extended. Rio: Record, 1999.

Capoeira, os fundamentos da malícia. Rio: Record, 1992.
Eighth edition, revised and extended. Rio: Record, 2002.

*A balada de Noivo-da-Vida e Veneno-da-Madrugada
(romance).* Rio: Record, 1997.

In other countries

L'ABC du joueur de capoeira. Paris: ATABAC/Gilles Cheze,
1997. Second edition. Paris: Ed. Budostore, 2002.

Capoeira, kampdans og livfilosofi fra Brasilien. Odense,
Denmark: Odense Universtetsforlag, 1997.

Capoeira, kampfkunst und tanz aus Brasilien. Berlin: Verlag
Weinmann, 1999.

Capoeira. Rijswijk, Holland: Elmar, 2002.

The Little Capoeira Book

Nestor Capoeira

translated by
Alex Ladd

Revised Edition

BLUE SNAKE BOOKS
BERKELEY, CALIFORNIA

Published by Blue Snake Books
Blue Snake Books' publications are distributed by
North Atlantic Books
P.O. Box 1232
Berkeley, California 94712

Cover art by Edson Campos
Artwork of movements, sequences and kicks by Silas Queiroz
Back-cover photograph by Zé Roberto (from the film *Cordão de Ouro* by A.C. Fontura)
Black-and-white photographs provided by Dr. Maurício Vinhas de Queiroz.
These photographs were taken in the 1950s, and depict the *roda* of Mestre Valdemar da Paixão
(striped shirt), one of the great *Angoleiros* of his time.
Drawing of Mestre Bimba by Bodinho, from the *Jornal da Capoeira*
Cover and book design by Paula Morrison
Printed in the United States of America

The Little Capoeira Book is sponsored by the Society for the Study of Native Arts and Sciences, a non-profit educational corporation whose goals are to develop an educational and crosscultural perspective linking various scientific, social, and artistic fields; to nurture a holistic view of the arts, sciences, humanities, and healing; and to publish and distribute literature on the relationship of mind, body, and nature.

PLEASE NOTE: The creators and publishers of this book are not and will not be responsible, in any way whatsoever, for any improper use made by anyone of the information contained in this book. All use of the aforementioned information must be made in accordance with what is permitted by law, and any damage liable to be caused as a result thereof will be the exclusive responsibility of the user. In addition, he or she must adhere strictly to the safety rules contained in the book, both in training and in actual implementation of the information presented herein. This book is intended for use in conjunction with ongoing lessons and personal training with an authorized expert. It is not a substitute for formal training. It is the sole responsibility of every person planning to train in the techniques described in this book to consult a licensed physician in order to obtain complete medical information on his or her personal ability and limitations. The instructions and advice printed in this book are not in any way intended as a substitute for medical, mental, or emotional counseling with a licensed physician or health-care provider.

ISBN 978-1-58394-198-0

The Library of Congress has cataloged the earlier edition as follows:
Capoeira, Nestor
[Pequeno manual do jogador de capoeira. English]
The little capoeira book / Nestor Capoeira : translated by Alex Ladd.
     p.   cm.
   ISBN 1-55643-440-5
   1. Capoeira (Dance)   I. Title.
GV1796.C145C3513 1995
793.33—dc20   95-2216
                                   CIP

11 12 13 14 15 16 17 18 DATA 14 13 12 11 10 09 08 07

This book is dedicated to Dermeval Lopez de Lacerda, Mestre Leopoldina, who introduced me to the mysteries and the *malandragens* of capoeira; and to all of the players past, present and future.

For more information regarding capoeira groups in your area contact:

The Capoeira Foundation
Jelon Vieira (Mestre Jelon)
105 Franklin St.,
New York, New York
10013
(212) 274-9737

Capoeira Bahia
Bira Almeida (Mestre Acordeon)
505 42nd Street
Richmond, California 94805
(510)236-8901

TABLE OF CONTENTS

A PREFACE BY THE TRANSLATOR

I remember seeing a capoeira exhibition for the first time as a small boy in a hotel in Salvador, Bahia — Brazil's undisputed capital of Afro-Brazilian culture. Two sinewy, bare-chested men took the hotel's stage and proceeded to awe that child with moves that until then I had thought were restricted to comic-book heroes — and all of this done to the infectious beat of exotic instruments with names like *berimbau, reco-reco, pandeiro, atabaque* and *agô-gô*.

As a college student, twelve years later, seeking to enroll in a martial arts class, I thought again about the exhibition that I had seen in Bahia. Why not study a martial art whose roots in this hemisphere were so deep and rich? But could it be that this unique art form was being taught in the United States?

To my surprise, I found that not only was capoeira being taught but that a burgeoning capoeira "scene" was developing in this country under the vigilant eyes of some pioneering Brazilian masters.

Among the first to come to the States and teach regularly, around 1974, were two young natives of Salvador with impressive capoeira credentials, Mestre (Master) Jelon Vieira and Loremil Machado (1953–1994).[1] Machado eventually gravitated towards performance and dance, while Vieira embarked on the difficult path of molding American capoeiristas on a par with their Brazilian counterparts.

A typical Vieira class in New York city during the '70s and '80s might include a Yale hockey player who could easily relate to this

---

1. Mestre Vieira was a pupil of Mestre Bôbô, Mestre Bimba and Mestre Eziquiel, and Machado studied with Mestre Nô.

THE LITTLE CAPOEIRA BOOK

mix of grace and muscle; an African-American jazz musician who found capoeira's African-structured songs a throwback to his own roots; and a classical ballet dancer mesmerized by capoeira's beautiful yet lethal movements. All seemed to find something in this unique art form.

In 1978, Mestre Acordeon (Bira Almeida), one of legendary Mestre Bimba's (1900–1974) leading pupils, arrived in California and began sharing his rich capoeira vision with his students there. He has been teaching consistently in the San Francisco Bay Area[2] ever since. His book, *Capoeira: A Brazilian Art Form* (North Atlantic Books, 1986) was one of the first published on the subject matter in this country and is still one of the best sources available for those wishing to learn the history and philosophy of this art form.

Soon there were many others, including the venerable Angoleiro Mestre João Grande, a former student of Mestre Pastinha (1890–1981), the foremost practitioner of the traditional *capoeira Angola* style of his generation. Mestre João Grande came to the United States in 1990, undaunted by his age and the cultural and language barriers he would face, and armed with the faith that he would communicate in the universal language of capoeira—and he was right. With the opening of his *academia* in New York City, where he continues to teach, he became one of the first capoeira mestres to have a school in the U.S. dedicated solely to the teaching of capoeira.

Add to those names Brazil's first woman mestre, Edna Lima (who also teaches in New York), plus several talented young Brazilian and American mestres and professors teaching all over the United States, from Boston to Santa Fé, who have all contributed in their own way, and all of a sudden we have a capoeira "scene."[3]

---

2. Today there are over a dozen people teaching capoeira in the Bay Area alone.

3. The list of Mestres I have mentioned here is by no means complete. Many other talented mestres and teachers whom I have not mentioned for lack of space have contributed and are contributing to the growth of capoeira

For all of this activity, however, capoeira remains a foreign word to most Americans, not unlike many of the Asian martial arts in this country in the early 1950s. Although Nestor Capoeira resides in Brazil, perhaps the publication of his *Little Capoeira Book* in English will be one more step in giving capoeira the recognition it is due.

With this book we have for the first time in this country a manual that breaks down basic capoeira moves, with the help of easy-to-understand diagrams combined with insights into the history, ritual and philosophy of the game. Anyone who has studied martial arts knows that it is impossible to learn from a book alone—you must also "do." This is even more true of capoeira, which is so much more than a martial art and which demands participation on many levels. Nonetheless, this book can serve as an excellent introduction, guide and reference for both the beginner and the more advanced student.

Part athlete, part bohemian philosopher and part scholar, Nestor Capoeira embodies traits that make him singularly qualified to write on the subject matter. Nestor, as he likes to be called, is a former student of the legendary Mestre Leopoldina (who in turn was a pupil of Quinzinho and Mestre Arthur Emidío). Later he joined the Senzala group where he studied under Mestre Preguiça (Vandencolque de Oliveira).[4] In 1969, he obtained that group's coveted red-cord and later became one of *Senzala's* leading members.

Nestor Capoeira combines the knowledge of one who has done (and is doing) with that of a serious scholar and chronicler of the art. He is a frequent figure at conferences on this art form, and has been the official chronicler of several national and international capoeira encounters. He has taught capoeira non-stop since 1969, has three books published on the subject, and was a pioneer in

---

in this country—people like Preguiça, Marcelo and Deraldo, to name a few. For a more complete chronology of the early years of capoeira in this country, read Bira Almeida's book, which was previously mentioned.

4. Mestre Preguiça has been teaching in the Bay Area since 1984.

introducing capoeira to Europe, where he first taught in 1971. Through Nestor's eyes we can get a sense of the historical perspective of capoeira as well as recent trends.

Hopefully, this book will help to inspire a new generation of capoeiristas in this country. For those who doubt that this art form can be transplanted to American soil, it is necessary only to see top American capoeiristas in action. They have internalized the capoeira vocabulary and philosophy, and have achieved the ultimate compliment when Brazilian capoeiristas mistake them for one of their own. Their mastery is achieved through incredible hard work and dedication. I hope that this book will play a part in helping to spawn more capoeiristas like them.

—Alex Ladd (a.k.a. Graveto)

Alex Ladd was born in Rio de Janeiro, Brazil in 1964. He began study- ing capoeira in 1986 with Mestre Jelon Vieira and later studied with Mestra Edna Lima. He currently resides in New Jersey, where he works as a free-lance writer and translator.

PREFACE

In 1971, while I was teaching capoeira at the London School of Contemporary Dance, I wrote a little manual and photocopied it for my students. I felt they needed some information on the history and philosophy of capoeira in order to understand what the *jogo* (game) they were learning in my classes was all about.

Those pages were the beginning of something that has grown in the last twenty-five years, which today is part of my relationship with capoeira and the capoeira world: I have since published three books on the subject in Brazil and now I am happy to see my first book translated into English and published in the United States.

Of course, during all of this time a lot of new research and information has been brought out, and many of my insights on the history of capoeira have changed. I have also grown a bit older and more experienced in the game—of life and of capoeira—and have had the chance to strengthen my links with players and *mestres* older than myself, capoeiristas I had admired when young and whom I now call my friends. These friendships brought with them a richness of information—philosophical knowledge of the roots and the ritual of the game—as well as shared experiences which spanned many years. This, of course, deepened my understanding of what capoeira is all about. I am happy to say that this new material is present in this first English edition, and I hope it can transmit this information that has enriched my vision of capoeira.

So my purpose in this "little book" is twofold:

1) to inform the reader about capoeira, its history, philosophy, music, ritual, myth and significance; and

2) to provide a practical method of teaching and learning that will properly introduce the beginner from a different culture to the capoeira game.

Capoeira has enriched my life, has opened many doors and given me unexpected opportunities in these last thirty years. I have observed that I am not the only one who has benefited from it, and I hope that the reader will shortly join our *roda* (circle).

—Nestor Capoeira

THE HISTORY

Camará, donde é que vens, camará;
camará, donde é que vens, camará?

Comrade, from whence do you come, comrade;
comrade, from whence do you come, comrade?

INTRODUCTION

In 1500 the Portuguese, led by explorer Pedro Alves Cabral, arrived in Brazil.

One of the first measures taken by the new arrivals was the subjugation of the local population—the Brazilian Indians—in order to furnish the Portuguese with slave labor.

The experience with the aborigines was a failure—the Indians quickly died in captivity or fled to their nearby homes. The Portuguese then began to import slave labor from Africa. On the other side of the Atlantic, free men and women were captured, loaded onto ghastly slave ships and sent on a nightmarish voyage that for most would end in perpetual bondage.

The Africans first arrived by the hundreds and later by the thousands. They brought with them their culture—vibrant and different from the European one—a culture that was not stored away in books or museums but rather in the body, mind, heart and soul; a culture that was transmitted from father to son, from the initiate to the novice throughout the generations.

There was *candomblé,* a religion; the *berimbau,* a musical instrument; *vatapá,* a food; and so many other things—in short, a way of life. This book makes reference to a small part of that vast whole—the game of capoeira.

ORIGINS

The origins of capoeira—whether African or Brazilian—are cause for controversy to this day; different and opposing theories have been created to explain how it all began. Unfortunately, the early days of capoeira are shrouded in mystery, since few documents exist from that era regarding capoeira, and research on the matter is still in its initial stages.

3

But so that we may better understand the subject, let us also embark on a terrible voyage similar to that of the slave ships as they carried their human cargo to a life of slavery.

Let us imagine the landing of a flying saucer arriving from a distant planet. Its crew members carry terrible and unknown weapons. A great number of people, among general chaos and bloodshed, are captured.

After the frightful voyage, we arrive at our new home. There we are sold into slavery, and after the first days of arduous work we are taken to rest in the common slave quarters. We get to know our companions in this calamity: an American guitar player, an English boxer, a Brazilian samba percussionist, a Chinese tai-chi practitioner, and an African *swat* player—among many others.

Time goes by, and during the rare moments of leisure we begin to absorb each other's culture. Our children, and the children of our children, are born and raised in this environment of heterogeneous cultures and enslavement. Let us imagine that gradually, over several decades, a new form of cultural expression is born—a dance-fight, a game that is a mixture of boxing, tai-chi, samba, American music and the *swat*.

Now we have an idea of how capoeira was born and what its origins were: a synthesis of dances, fights and musical instruments from different cultures, from different African regions. It is a synthesis created on Brazilian soil, probably in Salvador, the capital of the state of Bahia, under the regime of slavery primarily during the nineteenth century.[5]

---

5. Capoeira developed in other parts of Brazil also, particularly in Rio de Janeiro and in Recife, where strong capoeira traditions could be found in the nineteenth century. In those cities capoeira maintained only its original fighting aspect and did not develop the synthesis between ritual and fight found in Bahia. Later, in the beginning of the twentieth century, the capoeira traditions in these two cities were extinguished by the police.

Condemned to a whipping in the public square. Debret, 1834

DURING SLAVERY

Starting around 1814, capoeira and other forms of African cultural expression suffered repression and were prohibited in some places by the slave masters and overseers.

Up until that date, forms of African cultural expression were permitted and sometimes even encouraged, not only as a safety gauge against the internal pressures created by slavery but also to bring out the differences between various African groups, in a spirit of "divide and conquer."

But with the arrival in Brazil in 1808 of the Portuguese king Dom João VI and his court, who were fleeing Napoleon Bonaparte's invasion of Portugal, things changed: The newcomers understood the necessity of destroying a people's culture in order to

Jogar capoeira *or* danse de la guerre *(Rugendas, 1824)*

dominate them, and capoeira began to be persecuted in a process which would culminate with its being outlawed in 1892.

Why was capoeira suppressed? The motives were many:

- It gave the Africans a sense of nationality.
- It developed self-confidence in individual capoeira practitioners.
- It created small, cohesive groups.
- It created dangerous and agile fighters.
- Sometimes the slaves would injure themselves during the capoeira game, which was not desirable from an economic point of view.

The masters and the overseers were probably not as conscious as the king and the intellectuals of his court of all of these motives, but intuitively—by that intuition which is inherent in any dominant class—they knew that something did not "smell right."

How was capoeira practiced, then?

- In a violent form in Rio de Janeiro and Recife.

- As a ritual-dance-fight-game in Bahia, where capoeira progressively absorbed other African elements.

- Sometimes in hiding, and in other places openly, in defiance of laws designed to abolish it.

Capoeira at that time had little in common with the capoeira that is practiced today or during the last one hundred years.

Take, for example, a description by the German artist Rugendas. His drawings of what he called *"Capüera, danse de la guerre"* ("Capoeira, war dance") and his written description of what he witnessed (*Voyage Picturesque et Historique dans le Bresil,* Engelman & Co., Paris 1824) are some of the first records we have of capoeira:[6]

> The Negroes have yet another war-like past-time, which is much more violent—capoeira: two champions throw themselves at each other, trying to strike their heads at the chest of the adversary whom they are trying to knock over. The attack is avoided with leaps to the sides and with stationary maneuvers which are equally as skillful, but in launching themselves at each other it so happens that they strike their heads together with great force, and it is not rare that the game degenerates into a fight, causing knifes to be brought into the picture, and bloodying the sport.

Absent from Rugendas' description are the acrobatic jumps, the ground movements, the leg blows, and the musical instrument called the *berimbau,* which had not yet been incorporated into the

---

6. Confirming this version of a more violent early capoeira, we have a letter from 1821, from the Military Commission of Rio de Janeiro to the War Ministry, complaining of "capoeira Negroes arrested by the military school for disorderly conduct." The letter recommends public punishment as a deterrent, and states that "there have been six deaths attributed to the before-mentioned capoeiras as well as several knife injuries."

game of capoeira. The *berimbau* is a one-stringed instrument with a gourd attached; its simplicity belies the range of sound an experienced player can summon from it. Ironically, today it is often considered indispensable and indeed dictates the rhythm and nature of the game—slower or faster, more combative or playful, treacherous or harmonious, etc.

In those days, capoeira was accompanied only by the *atabaque* (similar to the conga drum), hand-clapping and singing, as shown in Rugendas' drawing.

As time went by, this early capoeira described by Rugendas evolved and changed, partly through the mere passage of time—everything changes with time—and partly through the influence of other forms of fighting and dance coming from Africa, such as this dance described in a passage by Curt Sachs in *World History of Dance:*

> Two dancers and a singer take their places in the center of the circle. One sings praises to the old chiefs and maybe also to his favorite bull, and marks the rhythm with hand claps, while the other two dancers execute acrobatic moves and flips.

Musicians and acrobat during an African burial in Brazil (Debret 1834).

8

It must be stressed that there are many other theories attempting to explain the origins of capoeira.

According to one prevalent theory, capoeira was a fight that was disguised as a dance so that it could be practiced unbeknownst to the white slave owners. This seems unlikely because, around 1814, when African culture began to be repressed, other forms of African dancing suffered prohibition along with capoeira, so there was no sense in disguising capoeira as a dance.

Another theory says that the Mucupes in the South of Angola had an initiation ritual (*efundula*) for when girls became women, on which occasion the young warriors engaged in the *N'golo,* or "dance of the zebras," a warrior's fight-dance. According to this theory, the N'golo was capoeira itself. This theory was presented by Câmara Cascudo (*Folclore do Brasil,* 1967), but one year later Waldeloir Rego (*Capoeira Angola,* Editora Itapoan, Salvador, 1968) warned that this "strange theory" should be looked upon with reserve until it was properly proven (something that never happened). If the *N'Golo* did exist, it would seem that it was at best one of several dances that contributed to the creation of early capoeira.

Other theories mix Zumbi, the legendary leader of the Quilombo dos Palmares (a community made up of those who managed to flee from slavery) with the origins of capoeira, without any reliable information on the matter.

All of these theories are extremely important when we try to understand the myth that surrounds capoeira, but they clearly cannot be accepted as historical fact according to the data and information that we presently have. Perhaps with further research the theory that we have proposed here, i.e., capoeira as a mix of various African dances and fights that occurred in Brazil, primarily in the 19th century, will also be outdated in future years.[7]

---

7. We say that the mixture of the capoeira described by Rugendas (1824) with other African elements happened in the nineteenth century, but when this original capoeira began to be practiced we do not know.

THE FREEING OF THE SLAVES

With the signing of the Golden Law in 1888, which abolished slavery, the newly freed blacks did not find a place for themselves within the existing socio-economic order. The capoeirista, with his fighting skills, self-confidence, and individuality, quickly descended into criminality—and capoeira along with him.

In Rio de Janeiro, where capoeira had developed exclusively as a form of fighting, criminal gangs were created that terrorized the population. Soon thereafter, during the transition from the Brazilian Empire to the Brazilian Republic in 1890, these gangs were used by both monarchists and republicans to exert pressure on and break up the rallies of their adversaries. The club, the dagger and the switchblade were used to complement the damage done by such capoeira moves as the *rabo de arraia* and the *rasteira*.

In Bahia, on the other hand, capoeira continued to develop into a ritual-dance-fight-game, and the *berimbau* began to be an indispensable instrument used to command the *rodas,* which always

A capoeirista delivers a deadly blow with his razorblade (Kalixto, 1906).

took place in hidden locales since the practice of capoeira in this era had already been outlawed by the first constitution of the Brazilian Republic (1892).

We now arrive at the year 1900.

In Rio, the capoeirista was a *malandro* (a rogue) and a criminal—whether he be white, mulatto or black—expert in the use of kicks (*golpes*), sweeps (*rasteiras*) and head-butts (*cabeçadas*), as well as in the use of blade weapons. In Recife, capoeira became associated with the city's principal music bands. During carnival time, tough capoeira fighters would lead the bands through the streets of that city, and wherever two bands would meet, fighting and bloodshed would usually ensue.

In turn-of-the-century Bahia, the capoeira[8] was also often seen as a criminal. But the players and the game exhibited all of the traits that still characterize it to this day.

The persecution and the confrontations with the police continued. The art form was slowly extinguished in Rio and Recife, leaving capoeira only in Bahia. It was during this period that legendary figures—feared players, *de corpo fechado*[9] such as Besouro Cordão-de-Ouro in Bahia, Nascimento Grande in Recife and Manduca da Praia in Rio, who are celebrated to this day in capoeira verses—made their appearances.

It is said that Besouro lived in Santo Amaro da Purificação in the State of Bahia, and that he was the teacher of another famous capoeirista by the name of Cobrinha Verde, whom I met in Bahia in the 1960s. Besouro did not like the police and was feared not only as a capoeira player but as an expert in the use of blade weapons, and also for having his *corpo fechado.* According to legend, an ambush was set up for him. It is said that he himself (who could not read)

---

8. *Capoeira* can be used to denote the art form or, as in this case, the practitioner of the art form (who can also be called a *capoeirista*).

9. *Corpo fechado* (closed body): A person who, through specific magic rituals, supposedly attains almost complete invulnerability in the face of various weapons.

carried the written message identifying him as the person to be killed, thinking that it was a message that would bring him work. Legend says he was killed with a special wooden dagger prepared during magic rituals in order to overcome his *corpo fechado.*

Of all the rogues who led the carnival bands through the streets of Recife, Nascimento Grande was one of the most feared. Some say that he was killed during the police persecution in the early 1900s, but others say he moved from Recife to Rio de Janeiro and died there of old age.

Manduca da Praia was of an earlier generation (1890s) and always dressed in an extremely elegant style. It is said that he owned a fish store and lived comfortably. He was also one of those who controlled elections in the area he lived in. He was said to have twenty-seven criminal cases against him (for assault, knifing, etc.) but was always absolved due to the influence of the politicians he worked for.

Later on, in the 1930s in Salvador, Mestre Bimba (Manuel dos Reis Machado—1900–1974) opened the first capoeira academy (1932), a feat made possible by the nationalistic policies of Getulio Vargas, who wanted to promote capoeira as a Brazilian sport.[10] From that moment on, Bimba began to teach capoeira in his *Centro de Cultura Física Regional Baiano.* In 1941, Mestre Pastinha (Vicente Ferreira Pastinha—1889–1981) opened his *capoeira Angola* school. For the first time, capoeira began to be taught and practiced openly in a formal setting.

---

10. Although Bimba opened his school in 1932, the official recognition only came about in 1937, when it was technically registered. It must be noted that the Getulio Vargas government permitted the practice of capoeira, but only in enclosed areas that were registered with the police. Vargas believed that physical education could be used to instill a sense of discipline in children if taught at an early age. He thought that capoeira, if transformed into a "sport," could help. In fact, much later, in 1955, he personally congratulated Mestre Bimba for turning capoeira into Brazil's "national fight."

BIMBA AND PASTINHA

The two central figures in capoeira in the twentieth century were undoubtedly Mestre Bimba and Mestre Pastinha. In fact, these two figures are so important in the history of capoeira that they (and the legend that surrounds them) are the mythical ancestors of all capoeira players, and much of what we are or try to be is due to what these men were or represented.

Mestre Bimba was born Manoel dos Reis Machado in 1900. He was initiated in capoeira when he was twelve years old, in an area known today as Liberdade, in Salvador. His mestre was the African Bentinho, a captain of a maritime company in Bahia. Bimba opened a school at the age of eighteen, but it was only in the 1930s that he opened his first academy, where he started teaching what he called "the regional fight from Bahia," eventually known as *Capoeira Regional.*

Bimba was a feared fighter who earned the nick-name "Três Pancadas" (or Three Hits) which, it was said, were the maximum number of blows that his adversaries could take from him. Nonetheless, Bimba espoused the *malandro* philosophy of "brain over brawn." He was fond of saying, *"Quem aguenta tempestade é rochedo,"* ("Only cliffs face the tempest"), which meant that if you are faced by someone much stronger than you, the smart thing to do is to run; but if he were to run after you, then you could get him unexpectedly—a typical *malandro* attitude.

With the opening of Bimba's academy, a new era in the history of capoeira began, as the game was taught to the children of the upper classes of Salvador.

Bimba introduced sweeps from *batuque,* a form of fighting in which

Mestre Bimba in his thirties

13

his father was proficient, and new *golpes ligados,* or connected blows. He also created a new teaching method based on eight sequences of predetermined moves and kicks for two players, and on the *cintura desprezada*—sequences of flips in which the capoeirista learns to always fall on his feet (see page 86). He essentially sacrificed much of the ritual and "game" aspects, as well as the slower rhythms, in favor of greater aggressiveness and fighting spirit.

All of this, added to the very important fact that the majority of his students belonged to another social class (meaning in turn that they possessed different backgrounds and values, and a different way of thinking than the traditional capoeirista, who belonged to the underprivileged classes deeply rooted in Afro-Brazilian culture), contributed to the creation of a new style known as *Capoeira Regional.*

In the years following the opening of his academy, Bimba had great success. He and his pupils performed in São Paulo, Rio de Janeiro and other major cities of Brazil. But in the beginning of the 1970s, dissatisfied with the official institutions of Bahia that had never helped him, he decided to move to Goiana (near Brasilia, the capital of Brazil). One year later, on February 5, 1974, he died in that city. Up until the last day of his life, he was active and extremely lucid. As a matter of fact, he planned to give an exhibition in a club that same afternoon. Although he had asked to be buried in Goiana, some of his former pupils got together and brought his body back to Salvador, where he had taught and practiced capoeira all of his life.

Many other individuals created and began to teach new forms of capoeira, but they did not possess Bimba's breadth of knowledge nor his personality, and these novelties disappeared just as quickly as they appeared.

With the advent of the *Regional* style, the traditional capoeira style became known as *Capoeira Angola.* During the time when the *Regional* and *Senzala* styles eclipsed *Capoeira Angola,* Pastinha and his group were practically the only ones that still preserved the traditional style, although some other groups were still active.

Vicente Ferreira Pastinha, Mestre Pastinha, was born in 1889.

He is said to have learned capoeira from an African from Angola named Benedito, who took the young Pastinha under his wing after witnessing him being repeatedly beaten up by an older boy. In spite of his small stature, at the age of sixteen Pastinha became a sort of a bouncer for a gambling house in a tough part of town. He opened his first academy a few years after Bimba's opened and, due to his charisma and leadership as well as his friendly way of dealing with others, he was able to attract a devoted group of pupils and capoeiristas that made his academy famous as a gathering point for artists and intellectuals who wanted to see the traditional *Capoeira Angola.*

Pastinha became known as the "Philosopher of capoeira" because of his use of many aphorisms. One his favorites was *"Capoeira é para homen, menino e mulher, só não aprende quem não quiser."* ("Capoeira is for men, women and children; the only ones who don't learn it are those who don't wish to.") Like Bimba, he was well versed in the philosophy of *malandragem,* and would tell of how he would carry a small sickle sharpened on both edges in his pocket. "If it had a third edge I would sharpen that one too, for those who wished to do me harm," he was fond of saying.[11]

Unfortunately, government authorities, under the pretext of reforming the Largo do Pelourinho, where he had had his academy, confiscated his class space. Although they promised a new one, they never came through on that promise. The final years of his life were sad: blind and almost abandoned, he lived in a little room until his death in 1981 at the age of ninety-two. He left many pupils, two of the most famous being Mestre João Grande (now teaching in New York) and Mestre João Pequeno.

THE RECENT YEARS

In the 1940s Bahian capoeiristas began to immigrate to Rio, and later to São Paulo and other cities. Nonetheless, until the 1960s,

---

11. As we will see later, Pastinha also spoke of how this blade could be attached to the end of a *berimbau.*

*Drawings by Nestor Capoeira, based
on photos of the Senzala group in 1970.
Top: Gato and Mosquito; bottom left: Rafael and Mosquito;
bottom right: Peixinho and Mosquito.*

the uncontested mecca for Brazilian capoeiristas continued to be
Salvador and the state of Bahia.

In the beginning of the 1960s, capoeira students from Rio's middle class, after studying with Mestre Bimba in Salvador, returned
to Rio and began a self-taught apprenticeship. Ten years later, the
Senzala school reached its apex with the capoeira *rodas* in the neighborhood of Cosme Velho and became the most famous group in
Brazil, practicing and teaching a new *Regional-Senzala* style that
would influence capoeira players all over the country.

At the same time, in São Paulo there was also a proliferation of
capoeira.[12] Intensive warm-ups and systematic practice of blows

---

12. Today that giant metropolis has one of the largest concentration of
capoeira academies in Brazil. By one estimate, there are as many as 1,200
academies in the state of São Paulo, many of them concentrated in the capital city.

were added to Bimba's methods. Soon, in Rio as well as in São Paulo, a new cord system inspired by the Asian martial arts was adopted as a means of attracting more students by giving a "clean" image of a new and organized capoeira.

For a while there was even an attempt to create capoeira competitions with championships, judges and rules. Although, at times during the 1970s, it seemed as if capoeira were going to lose its ritualistic, philosophical and game aspects, and turn itself into another among many competitive martial arts, after a few years the championships stopped attracting many of the best capoeiristas. Although such competitions still exist today, they are not generally considered to have any real significance in the capoeira world.

CAPOEIRA IN THE 1970S AND 1980S

In the 1970s and 1980s, capoeira experienced great growth throughout Brazil and for the first time began to expand beyond Brazil's borders. Salvador lost its hegemony or, more accurately, began to share it with Rio and São Paulo due to the migration of its elite young capoeiristas to these two capital cities and the development of strong local capoeira groups there.

In Bahia, the era whose most celebrated elements were Mestre Bimba and Mestre Pastinha came to an end at last.

These two masters and their contemporaries were succeeded by another generation in their sixties and seventies, such as the legendary Mestres Valdemar, Caiçaras, Canjiquinha, João Grande, João Pequeno, Gato, Paulo dos Anjos, Leopoldina, Suassuna, etc.— true connoisseurs and representatives of the capoeira

Mestre Bimba at seventy years of age (drawing by Bodinho).

practiced by the previous generation.

For a while, though, it seemed that the rich and valuable capoeira which they had helped keep alive was rapidly disappearing. Their values, knowledge and philosophy often did not jibe with the new technological era and the new capoeira landscape in which they found themselves, an era in which the individual is alienated and television represents society's highest form of cultural expression — not to mention the drastic changes that occurred in Salvador in the last thirty years, which have to some extent transformed the mystical capital city into a center for consumerism and tourism.

For this reason, one could no longer find the traditional *roda* of Mestre Valdemar in the Liberdade neighborhood. Many of the other mestres, disgusted by this state of affairs, no longer taught, and only very rarely did they play. The mentality had changed; even in the street markets it was hard to see a good player performing.

On the other hand, parallel to this retreat of the traditional *Capoeira Angola* style and its old mestres, the new generation of *Capoeira Regional* teachers that had come from Brazil's middle class were having enormous success in terms of money, number of students, status and media support.

Although capoeira was beginning to experience unparalleled growth and acceptance in Brazilian society, some argued that something was being irrevocably lost along the way.

Muniz Sodre (a.k.a. Americano), a capoeirista from the old guard, warned against these changes in his article "A Brazilian Art of the Body." Capoeira, "as it was practiced by the old mestres from Bahia, was an anti-repressive exercise. To play was a manner of overthrowing the seriousness of the concept of art, established by a neurotic system known as culture."

He continued: "Capoeira today faces subtler and more powerful adversaries: tourism, which changes the ritual into show, and the pedagogical obsession which tries to make of the game and art a sport with rules and regulations."

Article in Jornal do Brasil *announcing the release in 1978 of* Cordão de Ouro, *a film starring Nestor Capoeira.*

CAPOEIRA NOWADAYS – THE 1990S

After the creation of *Capoeira Regional* in Bahia in the 1930s by Mestre Bimba, and the great success of the Senzala group in Rio in the 1960s and '70s, which paralleled the creation of capoeira championships with judges and rules, it seemed that the traditional values of capoeira were seeing their final days. Although a few traditional *Angola* mestres kept on teaching, they were completely eclipsed by the new style that had its origins in Bimba's *Capoeira Regional*.

But unexpectedly, from approximately 1985 onwards, there has been a revival of the traditional *Capoeira Angola*. Fortunately, some of the old mestres were still around, and returned to the capoeira scene with great strength, bringing back roots and values that had seemed completely lost.

Today, we are lucky to find a certain diversity that enriches the capoeira movement. Besides the *Regional/Senzala* style, which brought great technical development in certain kicks and other aspects, we can still find great *Angola* mestres who, along with their own highly developed technique and methods, have added to the deep knowledge of the ritual, music and philosophy of capoeira. And among the new generation of capoeira teachers, who are now around thirty-five years old, we find many of the best interested in both the *Regional/Senzala* style and the traditional *Capoeira Angola* style.

A game of Capoeira Angola *during the famous* roda *of the late Mestre Valdemar (striped shirt).*

O JOGO (THE GAME)

Menino escuta esta toada;
o lance certo muitas vezes esta errado.
Na roda, quem já esta classificado
leva sempre o sorriso que desanuvia
o lábio, ou então um rosto
que é como uma charada.

Hey, young man, listen to this song;
what seems right is often wrong.
In the *roda,* those in the know
always come ready with a smile
that parts their lips, or with an
expression which is but a riddle.

("Menino escuta esta toada"—Nestor Capoeira)

YÊ, VAMOS EMBORA, CAMARÁ!

Imagine that you are in São Salvador, Bahia, Brazil's mystical capital of Afro-Brazilian culture. As you walk through the cobblestone colonial streets of the old part of town, you can feel the pulsating energy that came from Africa centuries ago — an energy which today is the basis for so much of Brazilian culture and everyday life. The weather is hot, and the sun's rays reflect against the blue and green waters of Bahia de Todos os Santos (All Saints' Bay). The light blue sky serves as a stunning backdrop to the pastel-colored houses that line the streets.

People are out in full force — after all, this is not a car-oriented city like so many of today's modern cities. Here the streets and sidewalks serve as a gathering place: a place where people meet, do business, chat, flirt or simply hang out and watch the crowds from one of the many bars that open onto the sidewalk.

As you walk along the streets, suddenly you hear an intriguing sound, barely audible beneath the hum of conversation and laughter. You are lured by this hypnotic music in the distance, and you decide to follow it through the crooked streets.

Suddenly you turn a corner and see a small crowd gathered in a circle. Men, women, teenagers and children all seem to be entranced by what is going on in the center.

You manage to squeeze through the crowd until you get to a small open space in the center. Surrounding this open space are a group of men who are clapping to the beat of the music. Some of them are shirtless, and you can see from the well-defined lines of their upper-body that they are involved in the practice of a very disciplined form of physical activity. At the same time, your intuition tells you that, based on the way they carry themselves, these men are involved in some sort of warrior culture or perhaps even a martial art.

Opposite them you see the percussive band creating the rich sound that first attracted your attention: Three men stand side-by-side, playing long, bow like instruments *(berimbaus),* and they are accompanied by four others playing an assortment of instruments that seem to include a tambourine *(pandeiro)* and a conga drum *(atabaque).*

You are both confused and intrigued. What is this you are witnessing? Is this a dance, or some sort of strange religious ritual? Congratulations, you have just stumbled upon a capoeira *roda* for the first time.

A RODA (THE CIRCLE)

Let us now move closer. Someone begins singing a soulful song, and all listen carefully:

> Boy, who was your mestre?
> My mestre was Solomon.
> I owe him wealth, health and duty.
> I am a disciple who learns
> I am a mestre who teaches.
> The secret of São Cosme,
> is known only to Damon, camará.

"The secret of São Cosme is known only to Damon, camará!"— make no mistake about it: What we have here is a fraternal order, an association whose rites, although openly displayed, have meaning only for those who have been initiated into the mysteries of the game.

> ... Ê arruandê ...

Suddenly you are surprised by the shiver that runs down your spine as you hear the men in the *roda* respond in unison to the singer's call:

> ... *Yê arruandê, camará* ...

Two men are crouched facing each other at the foot of the *berimbau*, with their heads bowed. They seem to be lost in their own thoughts, or perhaps in some form of meditation. They lift their heads and observe the singer as he continues to "lead" the *ladainha*. The chorus responds accordingly as the energy level and the magnetism of the *roda* increase:

> The rooster has crowed;
> —*Yê, the rooster has crowed, camará ...*
> Ê, co-ro-co-co;
> —*Yê, co-ro-co-co camará ...*

The singing and the slow, hypnotic rhythm of the *Angola* beat begin to possess the two crouching players. Their minds are free of stray thoughts and ideas. Divested of all extraneous thoughts, they feel as old as the ritual they are about to engage in.

The singer and chorus continue singing in call-and-response fashion:

> Ê, long live my mestre;
> —*Yê, long live my mestre camará ...*
> Ê, who taught me;
> —*Yê, who taught me, camará ...*
> Ai, the deceitfulness;
> —*Yê the deceitfulness, camará ...*
> Ê of capoeira;
> —*Yê of capoeira, camará ...*

The two men touch the ground with their hands and trace magical signs—sketched lines that "close" the body and strengthen the spirit. The singer continues to lead the *ladainha*, and then gives the signal that the game of capoeira is about to begin:

> Ê, let's go away;
> —*Yê, let's go away, camará ...*
> Ê, through the wide world;
> —*Yê, through the wide world camará ...*

Ê, the world goes round;
—*Yê, the world goes round camará* . . .
Ê, it went round; . . .
—*Yê it went round, camará* . . .
Ê, it will turn again;
—*Yê, it will turn again camará* . . .

The two players pay their respects at the foot of the *berimbau:* From a crouched position, they lift their torsos onto their bent arms while their heads almost touch the ground and their legs hang in the air. Slowly, with complete control over their bodies, they return to the initial position and they face each other again. The game has begun.

They realize that it is no longer their friend or training partner who is in front of them, but instead there stands before them a riddle that can present dangerous and unpredictable enigmas in the corporal dialogue that will follow. It is a dialogue made up not of words but rather of movements—exploratory movements, attack movements, defense movements, deceitful movements—questions and answers in the mysterious language of capoeira.

The players glide to the center of the *roda* with only their hands and feet touching the ground. Their relaxed and seemingly lazy movements contrast with the alertness in their eyes. The singer has finished the soulful chant known as the *ladainha;* the *medio* and *viola berimbaus* improvise and syncopate over the rhythm laid down by the bass *berimbau,* or *gunga.*

The two players are conscious of all of this—the sound of the three *berimbaus,* the beat of the *atabaque,* the *pandeiro.* They observe each other while they effortlessly stand on their heads, make moves reminiscent of a cobra or a cat or a dolphin. They are totally in the moment. Their present and past problems all cease to exist. They observe the moment with a crystal-clear calm and the photographic tranquillity of someone seated on top of a cliff observing the sea.

One of the *berimbau* players leads a new song, still in the slow *Angola* rhythm, and the chorus responds. It is as if all of the energy of the *roda* is channeled and propelled into the pair of players in the center of the *roda.* The energy level continues to rise.

One of the players advances, slowly and carefully, and executes a movement of attack; the other one dodges the kick by moving under it. In spite of the movements that appear to be in slow motion, both players are alert.

Suddenly, one of the players unleashes a kick as quick as a cracking whip. The other, however, anticipates the blow and dodges it effortlessly.

One of the two players spins on his heels and stops with one arm raised. The other one approaches him, swirling close to the ground, and holds one of his adversary's feet in check with his arms so as to prevent any treachery. He cautiously rises and touches his

hand. They walk backward and forward as if engaged in a strange mating ritual, each touching the other's hands ... One of the two breaks this *passo-à-dois* with a quick and sudden kick, but his adversary has already dodged it and is far away.

Now the *berimbaus* start to play at a faster rhythm, called *São Bento Grande,* and the game unfolds standing up. The players swing, break and feint. The blows are swift, violent and unexpected. The defensive movements are dodges, which can be used in turn to set up a counterattack in the form of a kick or a "takedown."

Suddenly, without warning, one of the players spins, stops and carefully approaches his opponent and shakes his hand: This game has ended.

But another pair is already crouching at the foot of the *berimbau;* they pay their respects and a new game begins, with the *berimbau* commanding the rhythm and pace.

A GAME, A FIGHT OR A DANCE?

The question you asked yourself when you first glanced through the crowd comes back to you: Is this a fight or a dance? Or perhaps it was just a *jogo,* a game?

The answer, of course, is that it is all three, and much more.

Capoeira is difficult to define. Somehow the examples just don't fit properly. And it is impossible to classify it in known and established categories—dance, fight, martial art, etc.

To our Western minds, accustomed to dissecting and classifying objects, people and events into specific and standard categories, it can be difficult to grasp and understand what this thing called "capoeira" really is. But if we cut ourselves loose from the demands of our intellectual minds, and just watch the game in the center of the *roda,* we will probably be able to intuitively grasp what is going on here: It is something that we have experienced before, as children, when we played and were completely absorbed by the games that we created with our friends. The key words here are creativity, improvisation, fantasy, beauty and imagination.

But that is not all. Just as important are ritual, danger and sometimes even violence.

So now that we have seen a capoeira *roda* for the first time and have begun to try to define it, let us delve a little further into the matter and explore the three levels of capoeira.

THE THREE LEVELS OF THE GAME

Three seems to be a very popular way of dividing the parts of the whole:

Some speak of the ego, the superego and the id.

Others speak of Brahma, Shiva and Vishnu.

Still others speak of the Father, the Son and the Holy Ghost.

Let us then divide capoeira, for didactic purposes, into three levels.

Keep in mind that these three levels occur simultaneously. However, in any given individual, due to his or her personality, knowledge of the game and level of maturity, one of the three aspects will manifest itself more strongly than the others.

The first level is related to the physical aspects: the fight, the dance and the competition. At this level, it is important to be physically fit, to have efficient and well-placed kicks, to be quick and have good reflexes. On this level, capoeira is an exciting game among warriors.

Most of the players who practice *Capoeira Regional* have developed this aspect to a very high degree, often at the expense of the other two levels.

The player who dwells almost exclusively on this level, though, neglects the ritual of the game, and ignores the roots of capoeira. He does not play the *berimbau* (or plays it poorly); he doesn't sing. He is interested only in playing capoeira, usually in a very methodical way and often in an aggressive manner. He thinks in terms of "winning" or "losing," and he worries about his image and what others will think about him.

As time goes by, the philosophy behind the game begins to seep into the consciousness of the initiate, and he begins to notice a second level to the game—which was always present but which only now can he see and understand clearly.

The first step in understanding this second level is to understand *malícia,* the knowledge of humanity, of life, of the suffering and the motivation and fantasies of human beings.

This is when strange things begin to occur. The sensation of "being there" occurs during a game, shivers run down your spine as you hear the sound of the *berimbau.* The novice slowly begins to learn about the ritual of capoeira: the music, the songs that have been passed down from generation to generation, the philosophy of life of the old mestres. Suddenly it shifts from being a hobby to being part of your day-to-day life. Wining or losing doesn't seem that important anymore, and you are concerned about capoeira as a whole and what you should do to preserve it in the future.

As time goes by, you begin to be seen as an expert, but you realize that you are only a beginner. You begin to see how the practice of capoeira is changing you and your life, and the opportunities that it offers—opportunities to meet new people and to be accepted in new social circles, opportunities to travel all over not as a tourist but as a capoeirista. You also see how it protects you, and makes demands of you as well.

You begin to think about the capoeiristas of the past, and about the odd inheritance passed down from master to student. Sometimes it seems that the game represents something greater, as if it were a reflection of life itself, a reflection of the way different individuals interact with one another, each according to his or her own personality. According to this vision, capoeira is a school where one learns a specific kind of knowledge: how human beings behave toward each other and play the game of life with one another. You feel this odd sensation that something is about to be revealed to you, the feeling you get when someone's name you cannot remember is "at the tip of your tongue."

And then ten, twenty, thirty years go by. You are now a master. There no longer exists any distinction between you and capoeira: You live it; you are one and the same.

You now possess the penetrating glance that is able to discern what goes on between two players, not only on the physical level, but also on the mental and spiritual levels.

You no longer feel the necessity or the urge to experience this or that new or unknown *roda,* and you no longer feel the need to measure yourself against someone who is said to be a great player. You have been around and have seen the "world go round" again and again, and you have established a network of *camarás,* young and old players who are spiritually akin to you and whom you meet again and again throughout the world.

Or perhaps as a consequence of the unfriendly acts and attitudes of your youth, you have become a lone wolf in your later years, admired and respected by the young and inexperienced, but avoided by your peers who have no interest in doing any sort of business with you.

Whatever the case might be, you will then have had access—to a greater or lesser degree—to the third and last level, which had been present all along, since the first day that you heard the sound of a *berimbau,* but which only now reveals itself . . . something that can be called "the mystery and the deceitfulness of the game of life," about which the old mestres tell funny stories and jokes among themselves, but about which they never speak with others because there is nothing to be said to those who do not understand.

MALÍCIA

The *malícia* which the capoeirista refers to is an indispensable trait in the game of capoeira. In capoeira, *malícia* means a mixture of shrewdness, street-smarts, and wariness. It should not be confused with the English word "malice."

It may be said that *malícia* has two basic aspects. The first is knowing the emotions and traits—aggressiveness, fear, pride, vanity, cockiness, etc.—which exist within all human beings. The second is recognizing these traits when they appear in another player, and therefore being able to anticipate the other player's movements, whether in the *roda* or in everyday life. The player who is *malicioso* is able to dodge under an opponent's kick and prepare for a counterattack or a takedown before the assailant finishes what he started. In everyday life, he should be able to recognize the real human being that hides beneath the social mask of someone he has just met.

Another aspect of *malícia* consists of deceiving or faking the opponent into thinking that you are going to execute a certain move when in fact you are going to do something completely different and unexpected.

The development of *malícia* is a never-ending process that is stimulated by playing the game itself, by observing others as they play capoeira, and by observing everyday events in our lives and in the lives of others.

Malícia sometimes is called *mandinga,* although the latter word has an even broader meaning, since it also implies that one understands the basic forces of nature and knows how to use them to a certain extent by means of rituals involving magic.

Although an understanding of *malícia* and *mandinga* are essential to becoming a capoeirista, many players get carried away with it in the greater scheme of things. They forget a popular Brazilian saying, *"Malandro demais se atrapalha,"* which means that when one tries to be too clever or smart, instead of confusing his opponent, he confuses himself. They lose their way as they come into contact with this type of knowledge. They get obsessed with being smart, smarter than others, and with being powerful, more powerful than others; they get obsessed with being famous and with having status. And they forget that we all belong to the same *roda,* and that one has to have friends, one has to have fun, one has to enjoy the company of other human beings, in order to get the most out of life.

THE ORIGINS OF MALÍCIA: THE SLAVE AND THE BANDIT

We have already given a poetic description of the city of Salvador and of the capoeira *roda,* and that gives us a good insight into the "game." But if we are really going to begin to understand capoeira we must also have another picture of it and of its Brazilian environment. Let us then visit the neighborhood of one of the most famous mestres in Rio de Janeiro.

Demerval Lopes de Lacerda, better known as mestre Leopoldina, is famous for his quick and very unique style of playing capoeira, as well as for his mastery of the *berimbau.* But above all he is famous for the songs that he composes, which are sung wherever there is a capoeira *roda.*

Leopoldina must be well into his sixties, but nobody knows his exact age. If you ask him, he will tell you that he is exactly 283 years old and that Zumbi, who was the famous leader of a *quilombo* (a village built in the jungle by runaway Africans who were enslaved from the sixteenth to the nineteenth centuries), had been his pupil and that Besouro, a celebrated capoeirista who lived in the beginning of the century, was his second-in-command in a capoeira *roda* held in the city of Santo Amaro.

Cidade de Deus, the part of Rio where Leopoldina lives, is quite a fantastic place. It is not exactly a *favela,* one of the shantytowns or slums that line the many beautiful hills gently squeezing the town against the sea. Cidade de Deus has certain amenities that one does not find in the *favelas,* such as sewer, gas and water lines.

34

Also, the streets are paved and it is not on a hillside. But other than that, the social and cultural environment is pretty much the same as in a *favela*. That means that authority here does not lie with the state or federal government or even with the police, who must plan a special incursion with at least forty or fifty heavily armed men just to go into the area.

Law and authority here are concentrated in one person—the man in charge of cocaine and marijuana trafficking—and the hundred or more persons that he commands.

Although Cidade de Deus is a small part of Rio de Janeiro in the 1990s, it is a good insight into the slums that exist in all big Brazilian cities, not only in our day but also as it must have been in the last century. Let us not forget that the gangs that rule the drug scenes today live in the same *favela* that housed the capoeira gangs at the end of the nineteenth century. The social situation has remained very much the same since then.

At that time, a very small portion of society made up of the Portuguese rulers and their descendants born in Brazil controlled nearly all the riches and power. We also had a slightly bigger part of society represented by what is today called the middle class, and finally an enormous mass of slaves made up of free men and women captured in Africa, and their descendants who were born into slavery in Brazil.

After Brazil became independent from Portugal it was the same aristocratic group that maintained power; for it was Pedro I, son of the Portuguese King João VI, who took his father's advice to take the power for himself before another opportunist could do so, and made Brazil independent.

In theory Brazil was independent from Portugal, but in practice it was completely under the economic rule of England, Portugal's European ally, which had a monopoly on imports and exports to and from Brazil. In the early 1900s, after World War I, and later on, after World War II, this same economic and political and social model was maintained, although the domination was no longer English but American.

Now, in the final years of the twentieth century, we still have the same basic model, with the domination exercised by the big trans-national or multi-national economic groups. Nothing, in fact, has changed much: Brazil is the tenth most powerful economy in the world, and at the same time it is third in the list of countries with the most unfair and perverted distribution of money and wealth. A great part of Brazil's income from exports goes directly into the hands of international and North American banks and funds like the IMF (International Monetary Fund) to pay the enormous debt that Brazil's government has accumulated since the 1950s, the bulk of which was incurred between 1964 and 1984, during the period that the military took power.

Why are we telling you all of this? It is only under this global view that it is possible to understand the corruption and lawlessness that exist in the Third World. And it is only by considering this perspective that we can understand the unwritten rules and bizarre ethics of capoeira.

Capoeira is the culture of the oppressed! It was created in Brazil, sometime in the eighteenth or nineteenth centuries, by men enslaved in Africa and brought to Brazil. It was further developed by men living in the underworld of banditry and on the margins of an extremely unfair society during the 19th and 20th centuries.

Only after 1934 was the practice of capoeira permitted, and only then did it begin to come out from underground and to be practiced by individuals from more privileged social groups. Even then, there was a stigma attached to capoeira and its past, a stigma that began to fade only in the 1960s and 1970s.

From the very beginning, capoeira had to struggle to survive, since all African cultural activity was repressed in the 1800s. Facing a stronger opponent who controlled the power and made the laws, capoeira had to learn to be flexible and avoid frontal confrontations, to go with the flow of things. Capoeira learned the guerrilla way of fighting when faced by a stronger and more established army. It learned the value of lies and deceit, of ambush, surprise and treason.

One does not block a kick in capoeira; on the contrary, one goes along with it, thus avoiding the blow, and then counterattacking if possible. One does not confront a man face to face, but rather pretends to be a coward, to ask for mercy—and then to hit the opponent when he lowers his guard.

Capoeira knows nothing of such words, valued in Western society, as honesty, truth and fairplay when facing the enemy. Such concepts are luxuries that are not available when you are slave to a master who goes to church in the morning and at night rapes young women in the slave quarters, not even considering them to be human beings but simply *peças* (literally pieces, or units with some economic value). In the capoeirista's world view, such concepts are to be employed only with those who have proved real friendship.

On the other hand, it was clearly understood by the enslaved Africans, and later by the bandits, that one should not merely prepare oneself to objectively win or survive. Life is much more than just winning or surviving—it involves the joy of being alive. So all of this—music, dance, creativity, improvisation, poetry, philosophy, and having fun—is part of capoeira too.

But what about the First World? Has capoeira, with its special ethics and way of being, any value for Europeans or North Americans? Here the situation is quite different, for a good part of the population has achieved an economic level that permits them to live in a reasonably comfortable way. But economic and material well-being are not enough. Life, as we said before, is far greater than that.

In that sense, capoeira can be a tool in the First World, a tool against the forces that tend to turn people into robots that do not think, do not wish, do not have any fantasies, ideals, imagination or creativity; a tool against a civilization that increasingly says one simply has to work and then go home and sit in front of a TV with a can of beer in hand, like a pig being fattened for the slaughterhouse.

THE MUSIC

My *berimbau* . . .
whosoever should hear it play,
their sorrow, the sorrow they feel, will disappear.
You shall create a soul that is always new,
you shall create a soul that is always new!
My *berimbau* . . .
but whosoever should hear it play,
if it be a maid, she will become engaged.
My *berimbau*,
he only brings happiness, my comrade,
Yê, é hora, é hora . . .

(*"Louvação do Berimbau,"* by Mestre Leopoldina)

MUSIC AND CAPOEIRA

The capoeira *roda* consists of the following major instruments: a *berimbau,* an *atabaque* and a *pandeiro.* It can also include other instruments which are often present but which are not indispensable for most *rodas:* the *reco-reco* and the *agô-gô* (cow-bell).[13]

THE BERIMBAU

There is much lore surrounding the *berimbau:*

• Mestre Pastinha tells how, in the old days, a small sickle sharpened on both sides would be attached to the end of the instrument in order to create a deadly weapon: "In the moment of truth it would cease to be a musical instrument and would turn into a hand sickle." Thus the instrument, like the game of capoeira itself, combined within it two antagonistic poles: music and death, dance and fight, beauty and violence.

• It is said that in certain parts of Africa it was forbidden for the young who cared for the livestock to play this instrument; it was thought that its sound would take the soul of the youth—which was still inexperienced—to the "land of no return."

• In Cuba, where it is known as *burumbumba,* it is used to communicate with the spirit of the dead ancestors (*eguns*) in ceremonies of necromancy (Fernando Ortiz, *Los*

---

13. *The traditional Angola roda* usually requires three berimbaus (high-tone, mid-tone and bass), and one or more *pandeiro,* plus the *atabaque,* the *reco-reco* and the *agô-gô.* However, depending on the *roda* and on the ritual followed by the local mestre, some will do without these last three instruments.

Instrumentos de la Musica Afro-Cubana, Dirección de
Cultura del Ministerio de Educación, Havana, 1952).

• The *berimbau* was also used in many parts of Africa and
Brazil during the nineteenth century to accompany chants,
storytelling and poetry (Debret, *Voyage Pittoresque et
Historique au Brèsil,* Firmin Didot Frères, Paris, 1834).

The *berimbau* creates the mood and dictates the rhythm and
nature of the game taking place within the *roda*. According to the
old mestres, "The *berimbau* teaches."

Along with the hand-clapping, the chants, the *pandeiro* and the
atabaque, the *berimbau* influences the players' actions inside of the
roda. Or, if you prefer, these attract forces and energies to the *roda*
which vary according to the beat chosen.

The *berimbau* is made of a wooden bow, approximately seven
palm-lengths long and three quarters to one inch in diameter.

Berimbau *player (Debret 1834).*

At its widest end, a small peg is carved on which to attach a steel wire. The other extremity is covered by a leather patch, which prevents the wire from penetrating and cracking the wood. Nowadays the wire is taken from the inner sides of old car tires.[14]

A dry, hollowed-out gourd, called a *cabaça* in Portuguese, serves as a percussive box to amplify the sound of the instrument. A wide circular opening is made where the stem of the fruit used to be, and on the opposite side there are two small perforations threaded by a ring of string which is used to fasten the gourd to the bow.

The *berimbau* is usually held in the left hand along with a stone, a coin or a metal washer (*vintém*), which produces one of two notes produced by the instrument, depending on whether or not it is touching the metal wire.

The sound of the *berimbau* is produced when the wire is struck by a wooden stick (*baqueta*) approximately twelve inches long, which is held in the right hand along with a small shaker (*caxixi*) made of woven straw. The sound of the dried beans or pebbles inside the *caxixi* enriches and adds texture to the *berimbau's* sound.

By either placing or removing the gourd on the abdomen, the player can obtain different modulations of the same basic notes. There are three types of *berimbaus,* and ideally all are present in the *roda:*[15]

- The *gunga,* which has the deepest sound, plays the role of the bass; it keeps the rhythm, and normally plays the basic theme of a certain beat without variations.

- The *berimbau médio,* or *de centro,* also known simply as the *berimbau,* plays over the basic rhythm of the *gunga;* it plays a

---

14. In the old days, animal entrails were used.

15. Mestre Bimba would generally use only one *berimbau* in the roda, and he did so in his LP record *"Curso de Capoeira Regional."* When he is singing and the chorus is answering, we see that he played his *berimbau* as the *médio* that it was (he plays the basic theme of the *São Bento Grande,* followed by the basic variation of that beat, again and again). But between songs he improvises as if his *berimbau* were a *violinha.*

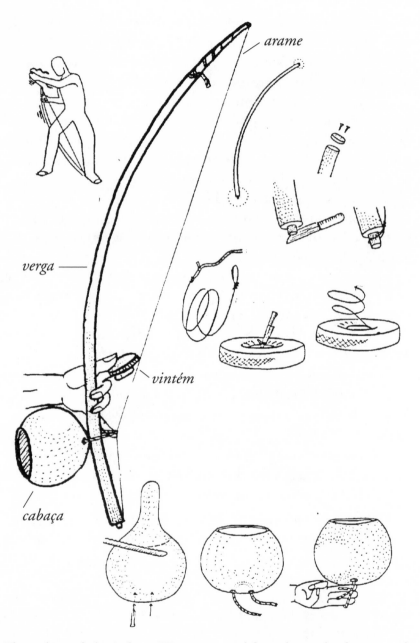

The making of a berimbau. *Wire is removed from the inside of a tire, and a gourd is cut in the fashion shown above, to serve as a percussive box which amplifies the sound of the instrument.*

role similar to that of the rhythm guitar. For example, it can play the basic theme of a certain beat, then a basic variation on it, and then return to the basic theme, and so on.

- The *viola* or *violinha* is the *berimbau* that has the sharpest sound; it is responsible for the syncopation or the improvisation. The role that it plays is equivalent to the solos of a lead guitar.[16]

The richness and intricacy of the rhythms make up for whatever melodic limitations the *berimbau* might have—when it is in the hands of an experienced player, one would never suspect it has only two notes.

The movements by the players inside the *roda* reflect the rhythms played. Depending on the rhythms or beats being played, the game can be either slow and treacherous, fast and aggressive, or open and harmonious.

There are many beats to choose from. Some are universal, such as *Angola, São Bento Pequeno, São Bento Grande.* Others are peculiar to one region or another, or were created by various persons. That is the case of the rhythms played by practitioners of *Capoeira Regional,* who play to the rhythms created by Mestre Bimba—*São Bento Grande (de Regional), Cavalaria (de Regional), Iúna, Amazonas,* etc.

THE CHANTS

The chants are not merely an accompaniment to the rhythms created by the *berimbau;* singing along with others in the *roda* is essen-

---

16. The use of three instruments with deep, medium and high-pitched sound is used in many African musical structures. We find it in *candomblé* (Afro-Brazilian religion), where three types of drums are used, except that the deep-sounding drum improvises (instead of the high-pitched *berimbau,* which improvises in capoeira). We also find this structure in Western music that has roots in African culture, such as rock-and-roll ("grandson of the blues") with the bass, rhythm and solo guitar.

tial to creating the necessary energy level required for the games to unfold and manifest themselves in the deepest and most complete way.

Also, within the three basic types of chants or *chulas*—the *ladainha*, the *quadras* and the *corridos*—there can be found a series of teachings, a code of conduct and the basic premises of a philosophical world view.[17] The *ladainha* is sung by the "soloist" before the start of a game, and is followed by a second part which is answered by the "chorus." *Quadras* are four-verse songs sung by the soloist and answered by the chorus. *Corridos* are one- or two-verse songs sung by the soloist and answered by the chorus.

If it can be said that "the *berimbau* teaches"—as the old mestres like to say—its teachings would be directed at the deepest reaches of the human consciousness.

But with the chants we find another, more rational type of teaching, based on the life experience of the elderly practitioners of this game. Let us examine a few verses of the *chulas:*

> *No Céu entra quem merece,*
> *Na Terra vale é quem tem.*
> *Passar bem ou passar mal,*
> *Tudo na vida é passar, camará.*

> You enter heaven on your merits;
> Here on Earth what you own is all that counts.
> Fare you well or fare you poorly,
> All on this Earth is but farewell, comrade.

> (Traditional capoeira song)

* * *

---

17. The *ladainhas* usually "open" or begin the *roda*. They are typical of Capoeira Angola.

Ê! Maior é Deus!
Ê! Maior é Deus!
Pequeno sou eu.
O que eu tenho foi Deus quem me deu.
Na roda da capoeira
Grande e pequeno sou eu.

Ê! God is greater!
Ê! God is greater!
Little am I.
What I have God gave me.
In the capoeira *roda,*
Both great and small am I.

(Mestre Pastinha)

Many songs are of unknown origin; others, however, are written by very well-known capoeiristas:

A lei de Murici:
Cada um trata de si.

The law of Murici:
I'm looking out for me.

(Mestre Leopoldina)

* * *

Não seja vaidoso
Nem precepitado.

Be you neither vain
Nor be you rash.

(Mestre Pastinha)

* * *

Era Bimba, era Pastinha,
Era Besouro e Abêrrê
Que jogavam capoeira
Como seu modo de ver.

There was Bimba, there was Pastinha,
There was Besouro and Abêrrê,
All who used to play capoeira,
All in their very own way.

(Mestre Lua)

Other songs speak about the atmosphere of criminality in which capoeira was born and developed:

Meu patrão sempre me dizia
Não fume desse negócio.
Se é de madrugada,
é arma de fogo e velório.

My boss would always tell me
Don't smoke any of that stuff.
If it's late at night,
You're talking firearm and a deathwatch.

(Mestre Bimba)

Then there are the songs that relate stories of encounters with "enchanted ones," with people who are possessed, and with the devil himself:

Tava lá no pé da cruz
Fazendo minha oração
Quando chegou Dois-de-ouro
Como a figura do Cão.

There I was at the foot of the cross,
Saying my prayer,

When *Dois-de-ouro*[18] arrived
Like the figure of the Dog.[19]

In W. Rego's excellent book entitled *Capoeira Angola* (mentioned earlier) we find many interesting chants such as this one:

Riachão tava cantando
Na cidade de Açu
Quando apareceu um negro
Da espécie do urubu.

Riachão was singing
In the city of Açu,
When a Negro arrived
Of the vulture kind.

In this song, the "Negro of the vulture kind" challenges Riachão to sing and improvise verses with him. Later it is revealed that he is the devil himself.

As is only natural for a game that is part of the vast and complex whole of Afro-Brazilian culture, many chants allude to *candomblé* deities, many times by the name of their corresponding Catholic saint. *Candomblé* is one of the religions the Africans brought to Brazil from their home continent, and it can be found in Brazil in its almost pure African form as well as mixed with native Indian and European cultures. *Candomblé* is the cult of the *orixas* (*ori* = head, *xá* = strength), or *orishas,* the cosmic energies that rule humans, the world and life itself.[20]

These *orixas* constitute a pantheon of gods similar to the ones we find in other ancient cultures such as the Scandinavian Viking

---

18. Two of diamonds; famous capoeirista.
19. Nickname for the devil.
20. Although *candomblé* is something apart from capoeira, in the past most capoeira players belonged to that religion. That is the reason we find so many references to it in capoeira songs.

culture or the classical Greek and Roman cultures. This song is an example:

> *Santo Antonio é protetor da barquinha de Noé,*
> *ê, da barquinha de Noé.*

> Saint Anthony is the protector of Noah's little ark,
> ê, of Noah's little ark.

Here the song speaks of "Saint Anthony" in the context of the biblical ark, but, in fact, it is referring to Ogun, the god of battles and war who is also the deity associated with iron.

> *Ai, ai, ai, ai, São Bento me chama.*

> Ai, ai, ai, ai, Saint Bento is calling me.

Saint Bento is said to protect against snake bites, and it is also the name given to two *berimbau* rhythms, São Bento Pequeno and São Bento Grande.

Among all the animals, the snake is the most celebrated one in capoeira songs, maybe because of its flexibility, and the fact that when it attacks it is quick, precise, treacherous and lethal. Here is one of the many songs that make reference to snakes:

> *Olha a cobra que morde*
> *Senhor São Bento.*

> Watch out for the snake that bites,
> Senhor São Bento.

It is very common for songs to guide the action of the players inside the *roda:*

> *Ai, ai, Aidê, joga bonito que eu quero ver . . .*
> *Joga bonito que eu quero aprender.*

> Ai, ai, Aidê, play pretty 'cause I want to see . . .
> Play pretty 'cause I want to learn.

And to leave no doubt that the chants reflect the action inside the *roda,* one needs only to hear the lyrics to the following chant:

Cabra correu com medo de apanhar ...
correu, correu com medo de apanhar.

The guy ran, scared of getting clobbered ...
He ran, he ran, scared of getting clobbered.

Another less obvious but equally important aspect of these chants is to allow the capoeira player who has just arrived at a *roda* to easily bring his energy in tune with the energy of those already there. He is thus able to relax and unwind the tensions accumulated throughout the day.

A more subtle function performed by the chants is that they allow players to catch their breath. Just like the swimmer who raises and dips his head in a rhythmic breathing pattern, the participants in a *roda* are also forced to enter a rhythmic breathing pattern as they respond in chorus fashion to the chants that others are leading. After finishing a game, many times tired and breathless, singing in chorus is a wonderful way to catch your breath!

LEARNING CAPOEIRA

Sou disípulo que aprende,
Sou mestre que dá lição.

I am a disciple that learns,
I am a mestre that teaches

TABLE OF CONTENTS
FOR MOVEMENTS AND KICKS

"I am a disciple that learns, I am a master that teaches." This quote from a well-known capoeira song reveals one of the most interesting and unique *fundamentos* (philosophical roots) of capoeira: The *capoeirista* always plays the dual role of both teacher and student, regardless of whether he is a beginner or an eighty-year-old master. He is always a pupil who is learning in the *roda* and in life, and he is always a teacher who is teaching, both in the *roda* and in life.

In fact, the real learning in capoeira occurs during the interaction between players during the *roda,* and not in the more structured instruction sessions. In the *roda,* players learn from each other—not only moves and kicks, but also strategies that are used in the game itself or in the bigger "game" that we play everyday in "real" life.

The players learn from each other, and those who are watching learn in turn from them. These varied observations of different personalities interacting with one another constitute an important body of knowledge about human beings, knowledge which also constitutes the *fundamento* or philosophical root called *malícia.*

In the "good old days"—which most likely were not so good—capoeira was learned naturally and intuitively; one would observe movements in the *roda* and try to imitate those movements. If one was lucky, one would find a mestre. Wherever a mestre would go, he would be followed by two or three apprentices. Now and then the mestre would give a pointer, and teach something.

Nowadays, times have changed. People have very little free time available. Mestres can no longer can be found wandering about. There are not many street *rodas* left where one can learn by trial and error in an intuitive, organic way. Capoeira nowadays is taught in the academies, each instructor teaching according to his own methods.

In the *Regional* academies, the teaching methods tend to be very structured; this permits a rapid development of technique, often to the detriment of improvisation, spontaneity and exploration of a player's individuality.

In the *Angola* academies, whose enrollments have been growing since 1985 after many years of being eclipsed by the *Regional* style, the teachings are more intuitive. The *Angoleiro* is almost always more flexible, has more *malícia,* and improvises more. Nonetheless, in the short run, the *Angoleiro* has a disadvantage, since the standardized technique and teaching method represent a decided advantage for the *Regional* players in the first years of instruction.

With the exception of traditional *Angola* mestres, plus two or three pupils of Bimba who are now in their fifties and who try to teach the original *Capoeira Regional,* what is now being taught in most academies throughout Brazil is a capoeira that could be called *Regional/Senzala,* because they use teaching methods developed by the Senzala group during the 1960s. These in turn build on the teaching methods developed by Mestre Bimba.

Thus, in today's classes, we see a lot of sequences of predetermined blows designed for two players which resemble Bimba's sequence. We also see systematic repetition of blows and movements done by many students at the same time as they follow the instructor's lead (similar to what we observe in the Eastern martial arts). And during the last thirty years or so, we have also seen the addition of calisthenic exercises, gymnastic and stretching techniques.

Nowadays we also see young *Angola* instructors who are teaching *Angola* but using methods similar to *Regional/Senzala,* with predetermined sequences of blows and movements as well as methodical repetition.

The ideal for a player who is already very advanced in his learning is to know and to practice both styles:

- to play *Angola,* with all of its ritual and *malícia;* and

- to play *Regional* (more accurately, *Regional/Senzala*), with its objectivity and its fighting spirit.

The beginner, however, in order to aid in his development, would do well to heed some of the pithy popular proverbs that are the essence of the *malandragem* philosophy—sayings such as *"Quem não pode com mandinga não carrega patúa."* ("He who can't deal with the *mandinga* doesn't carry a *patúa*."[21]) In other words, everyone should know his or her limits. Or: *"Urubu para cantar demora."* ("A vulture takes a long time to sing.") Another version of this is: *"Bater papo com otário é jogar conversa fora."* ("Chatting with a fool is a waste of words.")

Of all of the proverbs, though, perhaps the best one for the beginner to keep in mind is that *"valente não existe,"* which can be translated as "There's no such thing as a tough guy" or "the fearless do not exist." It is important for the beginner not to be fooled by the outward appearance of some "tough guys," and to realize that we all feel fear, and that we are all—to greater and lesser extents—insecure: "The fearless do not exist."

The capoeira player needs to see the human being hidden behind the facade of physical strength, whether it be in himself or in others. If this does not occur, then the beginner will guide his studies by a series of false precepts and stereotypical ideas, such as the macho tough guy, the deadly blow, or the notion of the superiority of one fighting art over another.

As time goes by, the beginner who guides himself by these false notions will turn into an idol of clay feet, an edifice with a weak base; he will have faith in the fighting techniques but not in the fighter; he will have powerful blows but lack faith in the person who delivers those blows; he will develop his muscles and his technique but not his spiritual strength. On the street, he will be able to beat this or that guy—but he will have to do this ever more frequently to reaffirm to himself and to others the image he is trying to impose. And once he runs into someone with a hot temperament and a cool head, he will crumble with the fear that his great

---

21. Magic amulets usually worn around the neck as a protection against evil and injury.

farce will be revealed for what it is.

In this increasingly violent sequence of events, he might feel the necessity to walk around with a gun, and he will then notice that others are also carrying guns. And the painful progression of his paranoia will be never-ending, transforming him into a coward who kisses up to the strong and the violent. It will transform him into the weakest of tyrants. All of this will occur because he didn't have the courage to look within himself and those that he idolized, because he was unable to see the human being within, in all of its manifestations both positive and negative.

PRESENTATION OF MOVEMENTS

We now leave behind the first part of the book, which dealt with theory. Let us now begin the section where beginning students are given a method of learning how to *jogar,* or play capoeira.

What makes this method a bit different from the methods that are being used nowadays and that have been used in the last fifty years (since Bimba created the *Regional* teaching method) is that it tries to combine the creativity and improvisation typical of *Capoeira Angola* with the structured and methodical training techniques of *Regional/Senzala,* which brought about great development in kicking techniques but unfortunately often made a player's movements resemble those of a mechanical robot.

We propose to do this by introducing the reader to a series of training techniques for movements of attack and defense through the use of diagrams and specific, concrete instructions and explanations.

When beginning any apprenticeship, the beginner often feels clumsy and foolish. He is full of good intentions, but after the first attempts he becomes discouraged. The student often rationalizes his difficulties by saying "I'm not cut out for this," and considers giving up.

This is normal in any learning process. However, we should try to educate ourselves so that we may overcome this inertia, this resistance, this fear of the new.

The beginner should allow himself ten initial lessons in which he puts aside all rationalizations and excuses for not studying and learning capoeira. I believe that after those first lessons the student will begin seeing things differently, and will realize that learning capoeira in order to play and be part of the *roda* is much easier and more fun than he initially thought. Of course, if he then wishes to achieve a high level of proficiency in capoeira, it will mean many years of practice and dedication.

Classes usually last one-and-a-half to two hours, three to five times a week. After the first six months the student should have conquered the first level of learning—he is now capoeira-literate.

I highly recommend that in the beginning students start with a master or a teacher who can guide them in the right direction. This is especially true outside of Brazil, where capoeira is just beginning to take off, and you cannot live and breathe capoeira as you can in Brazil.

It is also essential for the reader to keep in mind that capoeira is not merely the execution of moves and kicks. The final objective is to be able to *jogar,* or to play capoeira, and to do this you need other players.

THE MOVEMENT

Movement is basic to capoeira. Most beginners, and many advanced players, do not pay enough attention to this aspect of capoeira; they become so fascinated with learning different kicks or flashy new acrobatic flips that they forget this essential part of the game.

Let us explore three basic elements of movement in capoeira:

- the *ginga*—a form of movement standing up.

- the *negativa* and the *rolê*—forms of movement on the floor.

- the *aú*—a form of upside-down movement.

61

These movements are so important that I suggest that, before learning any kicks, the beginner set aside three classes just to explore them.

Students should seek out smoothness and harmony in their movements, and put aside the notion that they are studying a fighting style—this notion will only cause the beginner to tense up, and will cause his movements to be rigid, which is totally antithetical to capoeira.

The following exercise should be done to the slow rhythm of *Angola,* and some will gradually speed up to the rhythm of *São Bento Grande.* For those unfamiliar with the tempo of those two rhythms, we could say that the first corresponds to soulful blues and the latter to a frenzied boogie-woogie.

1. THE GINGA
(pronounced "jinga")

The *ginga* is one of the basic movements of capoeira. It is one of the features that sets capoeira apart from all other martial arts. Roughly translated, it means "swing" in English.

What makes the *ginga* special as compared to other martial art stances is that it puts capoeiristas in constant motion, making them a very frustrating target for an opponent.

The importance of the *ginga* cannot be overstressed. From the ginga the capoeirista can hide, dodge, feint and attack.

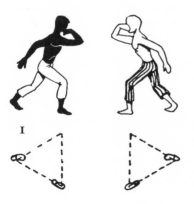

As a general rule, the *ginga* in *Capoeira Angola* is very free and individualistic. The ginga in *Regional,* on the other hand, is very structured, and its basic steps can actually be shown in a diagram form. This basic structure, however, does not mean that a *Regional* player cannot add his own style to these moves as he begins to master them.

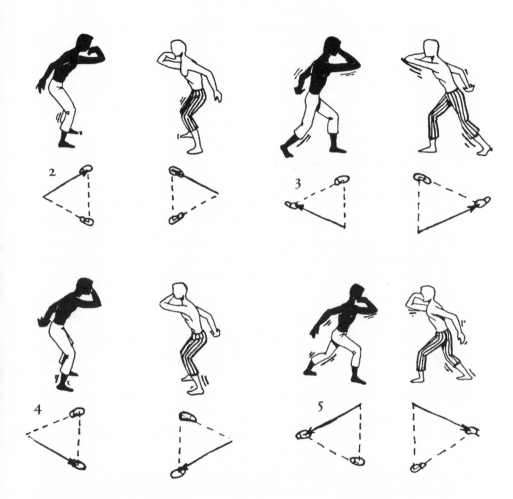

Exercises:

a) *Ginga* alone, as shown in the diagrams until you have assimilated the basic movements of the ginga.

b) *Ginga* facing another person, one following the ginga of the other as if looking at a mirror.

c) Movement improvisation (standing up): Now forget about the *ginga* and just move around your partner. Try to go around him. Avoid moving directly into him or cutting his movements short. Improvise your movements, and don't be ashamed of looking ridiculous. Your partner should do the same thing.

In this exercise, don't worry about synchronizing your movements with your partner. Forget briefly any preconceived notions that you may have about fighting. Relax and enjoy the dialogue of movements between you and your partner.

Move freely and try to react to each of his moves without throwing any kicks. Do not use the basic ginga in this part of the exercise; rather, use your instincts and your wits—you will find that they serve you well in capoeira!

Try to encircle your partner, putting him in the middle of a web of movements. This exercise is fundamental to avoiding a mechanical and robotlike *ginga,* which unfortunately is a trademark of many capoeiristas nowadays. Later we will explore movements of improvisation on the floor. These exercises are the core of this teaching method, and special attention should be paid to them.

d) Do the basic *ginga* alone. Then work with the improvised movements you did above by moving forward, backward, laterally and around. While improvising in this way, do not use the basic *ginga* movement. But after each series of improvised movements, return to the basic *ginga.* Eventually, this transition from improvisation to basic *ginga* movement should be seamless, so that an observer cannot tell when one begins and the other ends. Don't be tense; be relaxed and flowing. Let your arms flow along with you while you move. For now, do not put them in a fighting position.

e) Repeat the above exercises with a partner. When improvising, attempt to go around your opponent and to react to his movements. He will in turn react to your movements. Have a dialogue.

Note: With exercises a) and b), you will structure your basic ginga in the *Regional* style shown in the diagram. With exercise c) you will start developing your own personal way of moving while interacting or playing with someone else. With exercise d) you will start to articulate your personal way of moving, and blend it in with the basic capoeira *ginga.* And with e) you are going to play and interact with another person using your own personal way of moving blended with the basic capoeira *ginga.*

It is extremely important to understand how these five steps lead to learning the *ginga,* and the way that they relate to one another, if you expect to profit from the method presented here. This method combines the positive innovations brought about by Bimba's teaching method (combined with the contribution of the *Senzala* method developed in the sixties) with the creative and improvisational characteristics that are typical of the traditional *Angola* method of teaching.

If you understand how this is applied to the *ginga,* then you will have a clear insight into all of the other teaching methods and exercises presented in the following pages.

2. THE NEGATIVA AND THE ROLÊ
(pronounced "ho-lay")

Another distinguishing feature of capoeira with respect to most other martial arts is that the capoeirista is very adept at moving on the floor. Just as the *ginga* is the basic movement of the capoeirista when standing, the *negativa* and the *rolê* are his basic form of movement on the floor.

When the players move on the floor, they touch the ground only with their hands and feet, and eventually with their heads. They do not touch the ground with their knees, or roll onto their backs.

Going to the floor and moving there is part of the web of unexpected movements that dazzles the opponent. But the experienced player can also go to the floor in a real fight situation in order to lure his opponent into thinking that he is vulnerable and not realizing that a trap has been set for him. There exist a great number of kicks and takedowns meant to be used specifically in such situations.[22]

Last, but not least, moving on the floor makes the capoeirista familiar with the floor in such a way that he can quickly recover from a fall or even an attack, or take down his opponent from the floor.

---

22. Exercises for such situations are directed towards experienced players, and will be presented in Nestor's second book.

Regional *negativa*

Angola *negativa*

Coming up from the *negativa* with a *rolê*

Another way of standing up from the *negativa*

The *Regional negativa* is more erect; in *Angola* it is usually closer to the ground. The *rolê* can also be used as the transition from the *negativa* to the *ginga*, or from the floor to a standing position. In the diagrams we can see another form of "coming up" from the *negativa*.

Exercises:

a) Approach your training partner using the *rolê* while he stands still.

b) Move away from your partner using the *rolê*.

c) *Ginga,* go down into the *negativa,* change legs in the *negativa* so that your other legs is extended. (Important: Put weight on the hand that is on the floor when you switch legs, so that you spare your knees. Once you have switched legs, then proceed to switch your hands.)

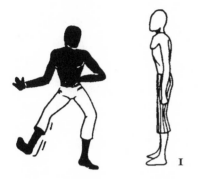

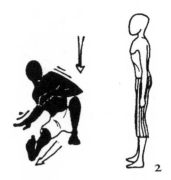

Moving away in *negativa* and *rolê*

d) After having changed legs in the *negativa,* try approaching your partner while he stands still.

e) Execute various *rolês* in a row.

f) Move on all fours, like a cat. Move forward and backward.

g) Move along the floor with one hand always touching the ground, like a monkey.

h) Move freely on the floor, occasionally using the *rolê* and changing legs in the *negativa.*

Note: In all of the above exercises, only the hands and feet should touch the floor.

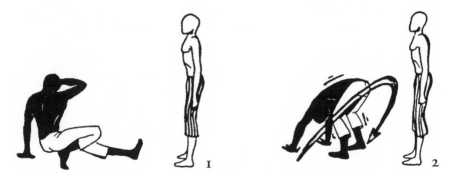

Approaching in *negativa* and *rolê*

i) Movement improvisation (on the ground): During this exercise, at least one hand should be touching the ground at all times. Improvise with your partner by moving around him and reacting to his movements, not by blocking his moves but rather by going around him and entangling him in a web of movements. When you see an opening or a hole, try to go through it by passing between his legs or under his body as if it were a bridge. When your partner tries to go under you, let him do it by creating holes through which he can pass. Do not use the *negativa*.[23]

In this exercise you should improvise and try to be creative.

This exercise, as well as the "movement improvisation (standing up)," are basic if you intend to be a creative player who really understands and is at one with the spirit of capoeira. You should do these exercises in a playful and relaxed state of mind, similar to what we observe when children play games on their own . This means you are playful and having fun but also completely concentrated on what you are doing and what is happening in the game.

A transition from the negativa (a) to the ginga position (f) by executing the rolê (b,c,d).

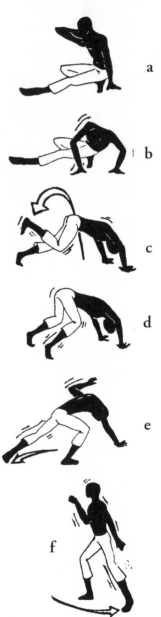

a

b

c

d

e

f

---

23. We do not use the *negativa* in this exercise, nor do we use the *ginga* in the exercise titled "movement improvisation (standing up)," so that the beginner will be forced to improvise and avoid mechanical repetition, which would occur if we were to use the *ginga* or the *negativa*.

3. THE AÚ

(pronounced "Ah-ooo")

The *aú* is known in English as the cartwheel. Through the *aú* the beginner learns how to find his balance while in motion upside-down.

Many beginners are concerned merely with learning fighting techniques, and in this context the *aú* may appear absurd. The beginner should avoid this frame of mind because soon you will learn the tremendously important role which the *aú* plays in the game of capoeira.

The *aú* is also part of the web of unexpected movements which encircles your opponent and leaves him dizzy, making him hesitate, lose his center of balance, and even open his guard. Learning to use the *aú* appropriately is one of the first steps in making the beginner comfortable in awkward situations that often arise in real-life fights, as when you suddenly slip, are thrown in the air or begin tumbling.

The *aú* can be an extremely effective way of approaching an opponent, or fleeing under certain circumstances. The *aú* and upside-down movements in general make the capoeirista very unpredictable, for it enlarges your spectrum of movement possibilities. The *aú* and upside-down movements also help the player understand that capoeira, and life, are not simply a matter of winning and losing; and that if life has many battles and struggles, you also need to learn how to dance, be poetic, have fun, be unpredictable (not always rational and objective), and be slightly crazy and chaotic, if you are to savor the best of life and capoeira.

In diagram a) we see an open aú, usually associated with capoeira *Regional.* In diagram b) we see a closed *aú,* the type usually associated with capoeira *Angola.*

As time goes by, the beginner will begin to master the *aú* in all of its innumerable variations, such as the *aú* with *rolê,* or the *aú coberto,* etc.

Eventually the player will feel as comfortable attacking and dodging while standing upside-down as he does standing right-side-up or close to the floor.

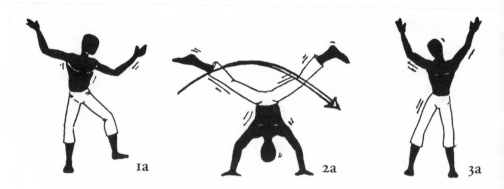

Exercises:

a) Try to do an *aú* to one side and then to another side. At first you will have trouble going to your weak side. Try to work through this, because a *capoeirista* should always be adept at going to either side. If you have trouble, try a very closed *aú* (i.e., with legs bent). It can even start off as a little hop, with both hands touching the ground for support; slowly your *aú* will begin opening up.

b) Practice the *aú*. This time be very careful not to look at the floor, but rather to fix your gaze on a person who is in front of you.

c) Practice the *aú* in between the basic *ginga* movement and movement improvisation exercises (on the floor and standing up). Eventually try to incorporate the *aú* into these movements so that one flows smoothly into the next.

d) Practice the *aú* with a partner using the basic *ginga* as well as the movement improvisation exercises (on the floor and standing up).

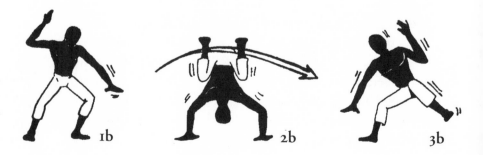

DEFENSIVE MOVEMENTS

During the first three sessions the pupil has begun to learn the basic forms of movement. Let us now begin to explore defensive movements. In capoeira, the idea is not to block kicks but to avoid them altogether. Actually, the pupil has already been introduced to one defensive movement, since the *negativa* and the *rolê* (basic elements of the ground game) can be used as defensive movements.

In an actual game each situation is unique, so the capoeirista must adapt each attack, escape, dodge, counterattack or takedown according to the circumstance that presents itself.

This ability to react intuitively according to the situation at hand is one of the most difficult to master. It is, however, a prerequisite to being able to achieve a good level of play. As mere beginners, we will limit ourselves for the time being to learning some classic defensive movements, and to incorporating these into the movements we have already learned. Later on we will understand how these exercises were the first steps in helping one to react intuitively to the situation at hand.

Eventually, though, you will see that while capoeira has some very efficient kicks for attacking an opponent, it becomes even more dangerous when the player is adept at using the defensive movements to move under an opponent's kick and then take him down, or to prepare for a counterattack for which there is no defense.

1. THE COCORINHA

If he is attacked by a horizontal blow (like a slap), the capoeirista dodges it by going into the *cocorinha,* with the weight evenly distributed on both feet. One of the hands protects the head, while the other can touch the ground lightly. This is typical of  the traditional capoeira *Regional.* Many times, as a player drops into the *cocorinha,* he gives a small hop forward, trying to come in under the kick so that he may get close to his adversary.

Exercises:

a) Do the basic *ginga* in front of a chair, and go into the *cocorinha* by taking a small hop forward. After going down, stand up and continue to *ginga*.

b) In front of a chair, do the movement improvisation (standing up) and incorporate the *cocorinha*.

c) Repeat the above exercise, this time with a partner; execute the *cocorinha* when you believe that the opponent is in a position to be able to attack with a circular kick or horizontal blow. The *cocorinha* is not suitable to avoid direct and straightforward kicks. (Note: There should be no kicks or blows for the time being.)

2. RESISTÊNCIA

The *resistência* is similar to the *cocorinha,* only in this case the weight is distributed unevenly between the feet, and the torso leans a little to one side; there is no forward hop, since the *resistência* is exe-

cuted when the opponent is already very close. As you will see later, the *resistência* can be the first step in taking down your opponent when he throws a direct kick.[24] The *resistência* teaches you to move to the side from the line of attack without retreating.

Exercises:

Similar to *cocorinha.*

3. QUEDA DE QUATRO

Unlike the *cocorinha* (where the capoeirista attempts to come in

under the kick), in the *queda de quatro* the player dodges, moving away his torso and

---

24. The resistência can lead directly to takedowns such as the *cruz* or the *rasteira.*

face while keeping his feet in the same location. From this position the capoeirista usually stretches out one of his legs and moves into a *negativa,* and then executes a *rolê* (in order to move in or away as dictated by the circumstances). Typical of *Capoeira Angola.*

Exercises:

Similar to *cocorinha.*

4. ESQUIVA

This is a very intuitive and organic way of dodging a horizontal blow, which consists of simply taking the head and torso out of the trajectory of attack.

Exercises:

Similar to *cocorinha.*

THE BASIC KICKS

After having completed the three sessions devoted to movement, and one to defense, we finally come to the fifth session where we explore kicks.

"Finally!" says the beginner. "Now I can learn how to kick some ass."

This euphoria, though, often turns into disappointment, since the first kicks are often done awkwardly and lack power. This is normal. Before you know it, though, you will have mastered these basic kicks.

Training sessions should from now on be done in the following sequence:

1) Initial warm-up—We haven't talked about this yet, but a warm-up session is a good idea before you begin your capoeira training. If you can do a warm-up using *ginga*, movement improvisation and a bit of stretching, that would be suitable. If you don't know what I am talking about, just run around and move for five to ten minutes.

2) Movement improvisation standing up (exercise c) of *ginga*)

3) Movement improvisation on the floor (exercise i) of *negativa* and *rolê*)

4) Practice kicks for one and two players. (Do only one type of kick per practice session for now.)

If the beginner does not have a partner for the exercises, he should do the exercises for one person only. With each new training session he will incorporate a new kick.

1. MEIA LUA DE FRENTE

In this kick, the outstretched leg moves in the form of an arc and then returns to its initial position. It is as if you were to pass an outstretched leg over a chair.

In the diagram we can see the execution of the kick from a lateral profile.

Exercises:

a) Practice the kick according to the diagram, passing your leg over a chair placed directly in front of you (ten times each leg).

b) *Ginga* in front of a chair, but this time you should be about five feet back. From the *ginga* position, take one step forward with your back leg and then kick with the front leg. Your foot should pass

1

74

2

3

over the chair. The kicking leg should be back when it comes down. Now continue the *ginga* movement and repeat with the other leg (ten times each leg).

c) *Ginga* accompanying the *ginga* of your partner (as if your partner were your reflection in a mirror); step in with your rear leg, and with the front leg execute the *meia lua de frente.* Your partner should avoid the kick by going down into the *cocorinha,* using a small hop so that he will end very close to your support leg. This exercise should begin slowly, with the person who is kicking warning his partner that the kick is about to come (ten times each leg). Later the exercise can be done faster without any warnings (when I say later I mean in a month's time, provided you are taking class or practicing three times a week). See drawings of Bimba's First Sequence in order to understand the kick (*meia lua de frente*) and defensive movement (*cocorinha*).

d) Later (in three months' time), the two partners will do the movement improvisation (standing up) and one of the partners will attack with the *meia lua de frente* without warning. His partner will avoid the blow using one of the defensive movements that we have already seen (*cocorinha, resistência, queda de quatro, negativa),* or by simply taking his head and body out of the line of attack by going under the kick.

2. ARMADA
(Armada Girando)

This is a kick that will take some getting used to for the beginner. The player steps across with his left foot (1); he spins his head and torso first until he is able to see the target (the head has spun about

180 degrees at this point), and then there is a corresponding spin from the feet (2). Only then is the kick released (3). It's as if the torso had "pulled" the leg like a spring.

Exercises:

a) Practice the kick according to the diagram (ten times each leg).

b) Practice the kick using the outstretched hand of a partner as a target. (Note: The person with the outstretched hand should place the target at the level of the abdomen. As time goes by, he will raise the target until it corresponds to the height of a person).

c) Do the basic *ginga* in front of someone who has his hands outstretched as a target; take one step forward so that you will be in a position to release the armada; execute the kick ten times each leg.

d) Two persons *ginga* accompanying each other's pace: one of them takes a step forward and attacks with an *armada*; the other person goes down into the *cocorinha* or *resistência* (ten times each leg); see drawings in Bimba's Seventh Sequence.

e) Three months after starting the training sessions, do the movement improvisation (standing up). Execute the *armada* without warning. Your partner should dodge it intuitively by going under the movement or by using one of the defensive movements shown before. The important thing is to avoid the blow (as opposed to blocking it) by using a classical capoeira defense movement or by using an intuitive defense movement.

Note: This sort of exercise, which is linked to the movement improvisation exercises and meant to be done three months after beginning, is of basic importance in this method. If you have read and thought about the different training steps in the *Ginga* section, you will understand that this is one more step toward a creative style of playing capoeira.

3. QUEIXADA
(pronounced "kay-shah-da")

The *queixada* is like the inverse of a *meia lua de frente*. It can be done in two ways: The player twists his torso, which is then used to "pull" the front leg, (sequence a); or, the leg is thrust forward, and thus the kick is accomplished with a small twist of the torso (sequence b).

Which kick you choose depends on the relative position between the two players. The basic difference is that one kick uses the back leg and the other uses the front leg. This kick should be directed at the side of the opponent's head, or at the opponent's cheek (*queixo* in Portuguese).

Exercises:

a) Execute the kick according to the diagrams.

b) Practice the kick using your partner's hand as a target (ten times each leg).

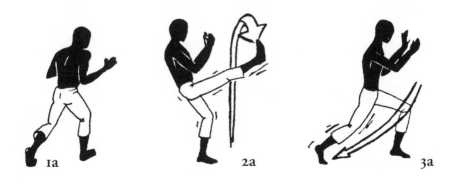

c) Take a step forward before executing the kick (five times each leg).

d) Do the basic *ginga* using a partner's outstretched hand as a target; take a step forward before executing the kick (five times each leg).

e) Two people *ginga* facing each other; one partner takes a step forward and executes the *queixada* (sequence a); the other training partner takes a small hop forward (which will place him close to the support leg of the person kicking) as he goes down into the *cocorinha;* he gets up when the kick passes over him and continues to *ginga* (five times each leg).

f) The two partners *ginga*; one steps forward and executes the *queixada* (sequence a), and the other intuitively dodges the kick. Take note that there is a correct side that you should go down on in order to avoid the blow (five times each).

g) Later on (after three months): Do the movement improvisation (standing up) exercise and use the *queixada* unexpectedly on your partner, who will in turn try to avoid the kick as best he can. You will execute the *queixada* twice (one kick with each leg) and then it will be your partner's turn to attack.

4. MARTELO-DO-CHÃO

This is a kick that is released from the *negativa* position. Frequently used as a means of attack from the floor against someone who is standing, it is more typical of *Capoeira Angola*.

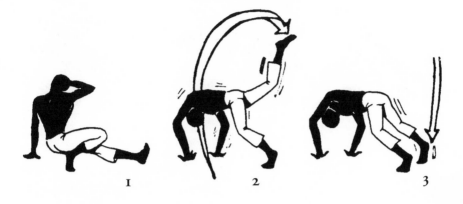

1   2   3

Exercises:

a) *Ginga,* go down into a *negativa,* execute the *martelo-de-chão,* stand up, continue to *ginga* (ten times with each leg).

b) *Ginga* somewhat at a distance from your target (i.e., your partner's hand), go down into a *negativa,* approach the target and execute the kick (ten times each leg).

c) Three months later: Do the movement improvisation (on the floor) exercise, and without warning execute a *martelo-do-chão.* Your partner will avoid it as best he can by getting out of the kick's trajectory.

5. CHAPA-DE-COSTAS

The *chapa-de-costa* is typical of *Capoeira Angola.* The kick usually begins with the *negativa;* then the player approaches his opponent in the *rolê;* then he aims for the opponent's face or groin area with the *chapa.* The *chapa-de-costa* is similar to a mule kick, and when it is done with both legs at the same time it is called a "double mule kick."

Exercises:

Do the movement improvisation (on the floor) using the *martelo-do-chão* and the *chapa-de-costas* as a means of attack. You will execute two kicks; then it is your partner's turn to execute two kicks.

Note: With the *chapa-de-costas* we finish our ninth exercise. We have already learned elements of defense and attack. The attack movements can be separated into those executed standing up (i.e., *meia lua de frente, armada, and queixada)* and those executed from the floor (i.e., *martelo-do-chão, chapa-de-costas*).

In our tenth training session we train the kick we feel is our weakest.

6. BENÇÃO
(Chapa-de-frente)

The *benção* is the movement shown in the diagrams (2, 3 and 4). Normally, the capoeirista takes a step forward from the ginga, in the direction of the opponent, and then releases the kick. (Sequences 1 and 2 show this movement.) The *benção* is an especially effective kick when it catches the opponent in full.

Many times the *benção* is thrown with a lot of violence; the initial step is transformed into an actual leap, and the entire weight of the player is used in the kick. In this case (this *benção* is called the *benção pulada*) the person throwing the kick will not have the control to be able to recoil the kick after it is thrown. If you miss the target, the tendency

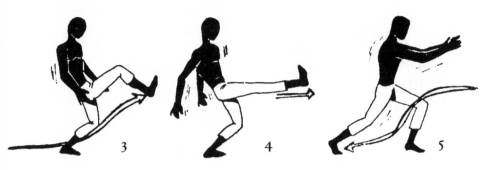

is to fall forward. Herein lies a lesson: In capoeira, when you attack in a very violent manner you are usually exposed to a counterattack if the kick is not effective. Usually, kicks that "go for broke" are a two-edged sword, not only dangerous for the person being attacked but also for the attacker himself.

Exercises:

a) Execute the *benção* (diagrams 2 and 5) standing still (ten times each leg). Notice that you are not really kicking the opponent but "pushing" him.

b) *Ginga.* Take a step forward and execute the *benção* (diagrams 1 to 5) (ten times each leg).

c) Practice the leaping *benção* against a punching bag of the type used by boxers, if one is available (ten times each leg).

The *benção* shown here is more typical of the *Capoeira Regional.* The *Angoleiro* releases the kick but does not recoil his leg and finish standing (as in diagram 5); instead, from position 4 he goes right down into a *negativa.*

7. MARTELO-EM-PÉ

A quick and explosive kick. The *martelo* is traditionally done using the top of the foot, but many young capoeira players have adapted techniques from different Eastern martial arts. Observe the movement of the arms (diagram 2), which helps to add explosion to the

kick and to assure that the kicker does not lose his balance. The foot kicks, and comes back quickly and under control. In the drawing we can see the player is stepping into the kick from the *ginga*.

Exercises:

a) Do the exercise according to the diagrams (ten times each leg). Do not go for quickness or explosion in the first exercises using the *martelo;* try to do the movement correctly at first, and the quickness and power will come with time (which could mean months or even years).

b) *Ginga* in front of a training partner with an outstretched hand, take one step forward and execute the *martelo* against the extended hand (ten times each leg). Note: Adjust until you find the right distance. Your foot should touch the hand when your leg is fully extended. The outstretched hand should first be held about waist-high and, as time goes by, the hand can be raised to head-level (this will happen months later for beginners).

1a   2a   3a

8. MEIA LUA DE COMPASSO
(Rabo-de-arraia)

4a

Along with the *rasteira* (which we will learn when we explore takedowns), the *meia lua de compasso* is one of the trademarks of capoeira. It is also one of the most efficient and deadly kicks. The kick is done with the heel (see diagram 3).

The beginner will execute the kick so awkwardly that it will be hard to believe that soon the kick will be fast and powerful. The *meia lua* usually begins from the standing *ginga* position (diagram 1a), however, it can also be used effectively starting from the *negativa* on the floor (see sequence b). An important detail is the position of the hands on the floor before executing the kick, as seen in diagram 3 of sequence b. The relative position between the person who is executing the kick and the target can be seen further on, in Bimba's Sixth Sequence.

Exercises:

a) Execute the *meia lua de compasso* as shown in the diagrams for sequence a) (ten times each leg).

b) Approach your target (the extended hand of your partner) as you *ginga* and release the kick (ten times each leg); note that the person executing the kick looks at the target in between his legs

(position 2a)—beginners often commit the mistake of looking at the floor when they execute the *meia lua de compasso*.

c) One month later: Both players *ginga,* one of the players warns that he is going to attack and then releases the *meia lua de compasso,* the other one dodges the kick intuitively (ten times each leg).

d) Three month later: Do the movement improvisation (standing up) exercise and without warning execute the *meia lua de compasso.* You will execute the kick, do some more improvisation and attack again. Then your partner will attack twice in the same manner. Defend yourself intuitively.

We've now arrived at the fourteenth training session, and have finished the basic kicks. In the last four sessions, the beginner has already begun to incorporate parts of the *jogo,* or game of capoeira, into his training session. If you are self-taught, that is, training alone or with a friend according to the method recommended in this book, the time has arrived to come out of your shell and get to know other capoeiristas who are more advanced (if you have not done so already). The time has also arrived to purchase your own *berimbau* and to become acquainted with it, first in an informal manner and later by learning the traditional rhythms used in capoeira games.

The beginner should direct himself to a local capoeira academy. As the saying goes, though: *"Pisando em terras alheias, pisar no chão devagar."* ("When walking in foreign lands, watch your step.") Limit yourself to watching the class at first. One can learn a lot by simply observing. Don't play with people you don't know, as a matter of fact, for the time being; don't even play with friends who are more advanced than you: *"Quem não pode com mandinga não carrega patúa."*

The decision whether to continue to learn alone or to join an instructor is yours to make. Follow your intuition. But as we observed before, the final objective of the capoeirista is the *jogo,* in the *roda,* to the sound of the *berimbau,* with other capoeiristas. Keep this in mind and before long, without even noticing it, you will feel perfectly at ease in the middle of the *roda,* playing capoeira.

BIMBA'S SEQUENCES

As I mentioned earlier, each teacher has his own teaching method. Nonetheless, ever since capoeira began to be institutionalized (in the 1930s) and began to be taught formally in academies, the use of prearranged sequences as a teaching tool has been common among many instructors. Unfortunately, it is now impossible to learn capoeira intuitively and as part of a cultural whole, as you could in Salvador up until about thirty or forty years ago. The times have changed, and Brazilian society has been undergoing enormous convulsions as it tries to enter the twenty-first century and to modernize its economy to keep up with the rest of the world.

Like everything else, capoeira has been touched by the changes surrounding it—and it could not be otherwise. In fact, capoeira is a school for life. It reflects life and the environment that surrounds it as if it were a mirror, as if it were a microcosm where the capoeirista can learn how to deal with life in a very special way.

One inevitable change, as capoeira has spread throughout Brazil and the world, is that the teaching of capoeira has become more structured. There are obvious reasons for this: Class enrollments have swelled, and teachers can no longer give the individual attention to students that they would like. Also, today's students often cannot dedicate entire days to the study of capoeira; rather, they often fit classes into very busy schedules, so they must get the most out of the short time they spend in class.

By giving the students rote exercises to practice, the teacher needs only explain the exercise once, and the students can then work together on that exercise. Also, it cannot be denied that practice makes perfect and that practicing a sequence over and over can produce impressive results.

There are, however, dangers with this approach. Many masters today, including myself, are alarmed at a tendency toward mechanical and predictable movements. This is totally contrary to the spirit of capoeira, which in its essence should be improvised and unpredictable.

In spite of all these changes, capoeira has survived and prospered, and remains an art whose "goal is inconceivable even to the wisest of capoeiristas," in the words of the venerable Mestre Pastinha. It is thus up to students and teachers alike to try to combat the forces that want to standardize capoeira, keeping in mind that the sequences themselves are not the problem; the problem lies in showing a blind subservience to these effective teaching tools. This can be done by creating exercises and methods that stress creativity and improvisation, as we are attempting to do here.

Of all of the structured teaching methods, in my opinion, Mestre Bimba's Eight Sequences (included in their entirety in this chapter) are still without a doubt one of the best ways of learning *Capoeira Regional*.

The sequences should be done from the basic *ginga* at a fast rhythm (the rhythm of *São Bento Grande Regional,* for example), although initially they should be practiced at a slower rhythm until beginners master the moves and can execute them without hesitating.

You should move on to a new sequence as soon as you have memorized the previous one, even though all of the kicks may not have been perfected yet. It will take approximately ten to fifteen sessions before you can complete all Eight Sequences smoothly.

The training sessions should be structured as follows from now on:

a) Warm-up;

b) Movement improvisation exercises, standing up and on the floor;

c) Exercises involving kicks: *Ginga* facing your partner, in synch with his movements; warn him that you are about to attack ("Now!") and your partner will then avoid the blow by dodging it. Do this with both legs, then trade positions with him (ten times each leg). Practice only one type of kick each session (i.e., *meia lua de frente, meia lua de compasso, armada* or *queixada*).

FIRST SEQUENCE

(In the diagram, we see the two players—"Plain" on the left and "Striped" on the right.)

Plain: *Meia lua de frente, meia lua de frente, armada* and *aú*.

Striped: *Cocorinha, cocorinha* and *negativa*.

1) The two players begin by executing the basic *ginga*. They accompany each other's pace.

2) Plain takes one step forward (left foot) in Striped's direction, situating himself so that he will be able to attack.

Note: At first Plain should warn Striped of the moment of attack.

3) Plain attacks Striped with a *meia lua de frente* (right foot) while Striped defends by going into a *cocorinha* (by taking a forward hop and going into a crouch near Plain's support leg).

4) Just as soon as Plain's right leg finishes passing over Striped's head, Striped
stands up.

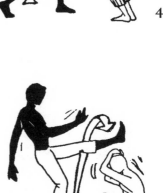

4

5) Immediately Plain attacks with
another *meia lua de frente*, this time with
the left leg. Striped goes down into the
cocorinha again, placing himself near
Plain's support leg.

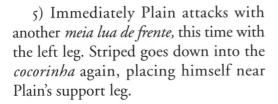

5

6) Plain finishes the *meia lua de frente*
(left leg), but instead of placing the left
foot back to its initial position, as would
be expected, Plain ends the kick by drop-
ping his foot forward, thus placing himself in a position to add an *armada*, which
will surely hit Striped when he stands up
from the *cocorinha*.

6

7

8

7), 8) & 9) Plain spins his body quickly and releases the *armada,* but Striped does not stand up. Rather, he goes down into a *negativa,* with the left leg stretched and the left foot placed in such a way that it could take Plain down by pulling on his left foot. Plain releases the armada using the right leg. Striped has already begun to prepare himself to come out of the *negativa* so that he can catch Plain when he escapes in an *aú.*

9

10) Plain escapes by doing an *aú* to his left. Striped changes sides on the *negativa* and approaches Plain, trying to give him a head-butt to the chest. Note: Come as close to your opponent as possible without knocking him over.

10

SECOND SEQUENCE

Plain: Two *martelos, cocorinha, benção* and *aú.*
Striped: Two *bandas, armada, negativa* and head-butt.

1) Plain and striped *ginga* facing each other, and accompany each other's pace. Striped notices that Plain is going to attack him with a *martelo.*

2) Plain steps forward and to the outside in an attempt to set up his *martelo.* Striped, however, anticipates his movement and attempts to take him down with a *banda* (a standing sweep, which will be explained in the section of the book devoted to takedowns). Plain releases his *martelo,* but does not find his target. Striped's foot is set behind Plain's support leg, ready to sweep; however, he refrains from taking him down.

3) Plain completes the *martelo* with the right leg, and after returning to the ground with his right foot, quickly goes into a *martelo* with his left foot. Striped again anticipates his movement, and again positions himself for the *banda,* where he could easily take Plain down.

4) Striped takes his right foot out, and quickly turns his body to go into an *armada.* Plain has already finished his left *martelo,* and is in a position to defend himself.

5) Striped releases the left *armada,* but Plain dodges the kick by going into a *cocorinha.*

6) Striped's *armada* has just passed over Plain's head when Plain stands up and goes into a *benção.*

7) Plain executes the *benção* with his right leg, and Striped goes down into the *negativa* (right leg outstretched), trying to set his right foot behind Plain's support leg.

7

8) Plain recoils his *benção* and prepares to go into an *aú*. Striped prepares to go into a *rolê*, which will position him for a head-butt.

8

9) Plain executes the *aú*, while Striped comes in for the head butt.

9

THIRD SEQUENCE

Plain: *Queixada, queixada, cocorinha, benção* and *aú*.
Striped: *Cocorinha, cocorinha, armada, negativa, rolê* and
cabeçada.

1) Both players *ginga*. Plain arrives at the point in his *ginga* where he would normally pull the right leg back.

I

2) Instead, he steps forward with his right leg.

2

3) Plain attacks with a right *queixada*. Striped, however, avoids the kick by falling into the *cocorinha*.

3

4) The kick passes over Striped, who then stands up, already inside of Plain's guard. In a game, Striped would have the clear advantage at this point.

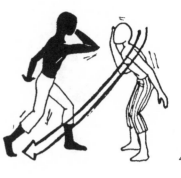

4

5) Plain recovers and immediately attacks with another *queixada,* this time using his left leg to kick. Striped again takes a small hop forward while going down into the *cocorinha,* thus putting himself near Plain's support leg.

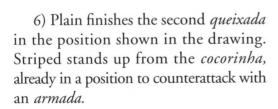

5

6) Plain finishes the second *queixada* in the position shown in the drawing. Striped stands up from the *cocorinha,* already in a position to counterattack with an *armada.*

6

7) Striped spins his body quickly and releases a right *armada*. Plain, however, has already gone down into the *cocorinha,* thus evading Striped's *armada.*

8) Plain stands up from the *cocorinha* ready to execute the *benção.* Striped, however, has already finished the *armada* and quickly goes into a *negativa.*

9) Plain would suffer an ugly fall were Striped to pull his support leg.

10) Plain escapes with an *aú* to his left. Striped responds by trying a *cabeçada.*

FOURTH SEQUENCE

Plain: *Galopante, negativa* and *rolê*.
Striped: *Arrastão* and *aú*.

1) Plain and Striped *ginga.* In this sequence we will encounter some moves that we have not yet covered: the *galopante* (an open-handed blow that targets the opponent's ear) and the *arrastão* (which we will review in the takedown section).

2) Plain steps forward and attacks with a right-handed *galopante.* Striped steps in with the right foot, and strikes his shoulder against Plain's hip while pulling him from behind the knees, thus knocking him down.

3) Plain falls to the ground, and Striped pulls the right foot in.

4) Plain was able to fall in the *negativa* position, but Striped is already getting ready to escape into an *aú*.

5) Plain uses the *rolê* in order to follow Striped and strike him with a headbutt.

FIFTH SEQUENCE

Plain: *Giro, joelhada* and *aú.*
Striped: *Arpão de cabeça, negativa* and *cabeçada.*

1) Both players *ginga* accompanying each other.

2

I

2) Plain spins on his heels (*giro*), threatening to throw a kick. Striped reacts by going down into a *cocorinha,* since he is anticipating an *armada* that is never released. He then goes into an *arpão-de-cabeça:* a violent move using the body's entire forward momentum to deliver a head-butt to the abdomen of the opponent. Striped places both arms in front of his face in order to protect it in case of a counterattack, while delivering the head-butt.

3) Plain releases a *joelhada* (a knee blow) aimed at Striped's face. Striped retreats into a *negativa* without having completed the *cabeçada.*

3

99

4) & 5) Plain prepares to escape with an *aú*. Striped should follow Plain in a *rolê* so that he can strike him with a head-butt.

4

5

SIXTH SEQUENCE

Plain: *Meia lua de compasso* and *cocorinha*.
Striped: *Cocorinha* and *meia lua de
compasso*.

1) Both players *ginga* at the same pace.
Plain prepares to go into a *meia lua*.

2) Plain steps in with his left foot in
order to set up a *meia lua de compasso*
with his right foot.

3) Plain executes the *meia lua* and
Striped defends by going into the *cocorinha*.

4) Plain finishes the kick. Striped, from the *cocorinha,* has already taken a step forward with his right foot in order to set up a counterattack with the left leg in a *meia lua de compasso.*

4

5) Striped executes the counterattack with the left leg, and Plain goes down into a *cocorinha.*

5

SEVENTH SEQUENCE

Plain: *Armada, cocorinha, benção* and *aú*.
Striped: *Cocorinha, armada* and *negativa*.

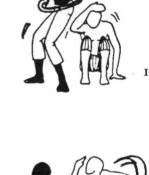

1) The diagram shows the training partners already in full swing: From the *ginga,* Plain took a step forward with his left foot and is ready to release a right-footed *armada*. Striped responds by going down into a *cocorinha*.

I

2) Striped stands up while simultaneously stepping in with his right foot in order to release a left-footed *armada*. Plain has not yet completed his kick when Striped begins his counterattack.

2

3) Striped releases his counterattack, a left *armada*. Plain had already completed his kick quickly, and entered into a *cocorinha*.

3

4) Plain stands up with a *benção,* and Striped places his outstretched foot in the *negativa* position behind Plain's support leg to prepare for a sweep.

4

5) Plain prepares to escape in an *aú.* Striped changes legs in the *negativa,* and approaches to deliver a head-butt. Plain escapes in an *aú.*

5

EIGHTH SEQUENCE

Plain: *Bênção* and *aú*.
Striped: *Negativa, rolê* and *cabeçada*.

1) Both partners *ginga* at the same pace. Plain steps in quickly with a *bênção*. Striped goes down into a *negativa*.

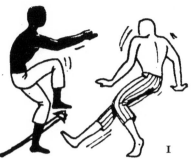

2) Plain executes the *bênção*. Striped, while in the *negativa*, has already placed his front foot behind Plain's support leg.

3) Plain escapes in an *aú*, while Striped uses the *rolê* to come in and execute a *cabeçada*.

Note: Always execute the Eighth Sequence at a fast pace *(São Bento Grande de Regional)*.
Do all exercises using first one foot and then the other.

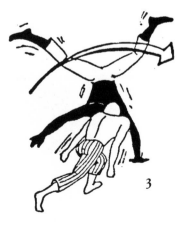

CINTURA DESPREZADA

The *cintura desprezada* is a sequence of four acrobatic exercises created by Mestre Bimba, wherein the capoeirista learns to always fall on his feet. As the name indicates (*cintura desprezada* means "scorned hip"), the old master felt that not enough attention was paid to the *"jogo de cintura,"* or hip movement.

a

a*

b

b*

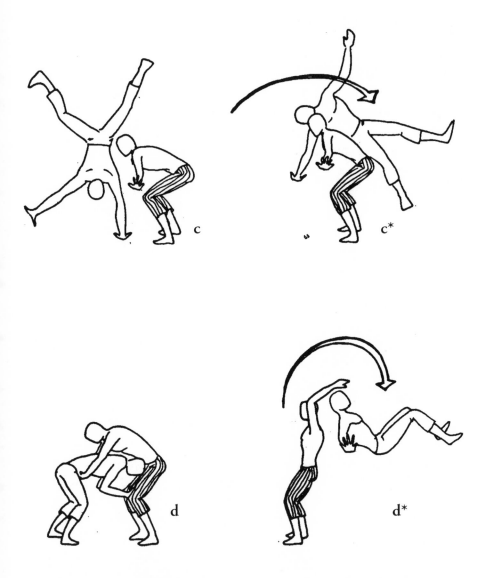

c

c*

d

d*

It must be stressed that these exercises should be done only under the supervision of an experienced teacher, so as to avoid injuries. Also, we must note that the person who is throwing his partner has an important role to play in helping make sure that his partner lands properly.

TAKEDOWNS

The beginner already has a sufficient amount of moves and kicks in order to be able to develop his game. Nonetheless, there are times when, in spite of a lot of hard work, the student does not see any progress—many times it even seems that the student is "unlearning." It is normal in capoeira (once the basic learning phase is over) for progress to come in spurts. You will go for months without seeing any apparent progress, and suddenly, when you least expect it, you jump to a new level in your game.

Nonetheless, you still have to be introduced to the most subtle, the most refined, the most efficient and without a doubt the most dangerous (for the opponent, of course) part of the game: takedowns.

The good capoeirista can play the game both standing up and on the ground; he knows how to play *Regional* and *Angola;* he composes songs, plays the *berimbau,* the *pandeiro* and the *atabaque.* He knows the history, the philosophy and the ritual of capoeira.

The exceptional capoeirista does that and much more: He is an expert in taking his opponent down; he knows and has mastered the secrets of the *rasteira,* the many types of *bandas,* the *tesoura* and the *entradas.* He takes literally the popular proverb that says: "The harder they come, the harder they fall."

As a matter of fact, I start to teach and practice the takedowns only about six months (or even a year) after the beginner has started to learn capoeira. I do not teach them one a day, as we have been doing with the basic kicks and with the sequences, but spend one or two weeks practicing a single takedown before moving on to the next one. Takedowns require a new and higher level of understanding of capoeira, and the learning process should be slow enough that the student can savor this new insight.

1. RASTEIRA

Along with the *meia lua de compasso,* this sweep is one of capoeira's trademark movements. When you understand the *rasteira* you are very close to understanding the philosophy behind the art form known as capoeira. Whoever has mastered its movement and knows how to execute it within the fraction of a second when he is attacked, will know how to overcome the most violent and aggressive opponent.

The *rasteira* represents the victory of knowledge over brute force, of shrewdness over strength. It is the weapon of the weak against the strong, of the oppressed against the oppressor.

As with all of the takedowns, the *rasteira* is executed by the capoeirista when he is attacked. Therein lies the difficulty in mastering the art of the takedown: In the heat of the game, the capoeirista is attacked quickly and violently, and there is no time to think or hesitate. Intuitively, he goes into the *rasteira,* simultaneously dodging the attack and pulling the support leg of the aggressor.

The fall is not pretty. Usually, when the *rasteira* is well-executed, the attacker falls on his back and—if he is not a capoeirista—it is not unusual for the back of his head to hit the floor, which can be very dangerous indeed.[25] By doing the following exercises, the beginner will learn to do the *rasteira* instinctively.

Exercises:

a) Practice the movement as shown in the diagram (ten times each leg);

b) Execute the *rasteira* from the basic *ginga* (ten times each leg);

c) Both players *ginga,* one attacking with the *benção* and the other defending and counterattacking with the *rasteira* (ten times each leg); in this exercise the person who is doing the takedowns should only go down into the *rasteira* and place the foot. If you were to pull each time, your partner's shin would never be able to withstand it. Toward the end of the training session, try pulling the *rasteira* two or three times just to see if it is working.

---

25. The way to avoid this, if you fall with your back to the floor, is to tuck your chin into your chest.

2. BANDA
(Banda de frente, Rasteira em pé)

We have already seen the *banda de frente* in Bimba's Second Sequence. The *banda* is frequently used against the *martelo* or similar direct kicks. It can also be applied when the opponent is not attacking, as long as the opponent has most of his weight on the leg to which you apply the *banda.* This type of *banda,* however, is rarely successful.

After having set your foot behind the opponent's support leg you usually twist your body to generate torque so as to sweep that foot off the ground. This is sometimes known as a *rasteira em pé.*

Exercises:

a) *Ginga* in front of a person who is standing, and step into the *banda* without completing the sweep (ten times each leg).

b) Repeat above exercise, this time executing the sweep. It may be advisable to use a shin guard for this exercise, although in a well-executed *banda* there should be no contact between the shins — the opponent's foot is simply swept out from under him.

c) Both partners *ginga,* one attacking with a *martelo* and the other reacting with the *banda.* At first, the person who is executing the *martelo* will announce that he is about to kick, but after a few sessions the martelo should be executed without any warning. Only try to take him down during the last few kicks (twenty times each leg).

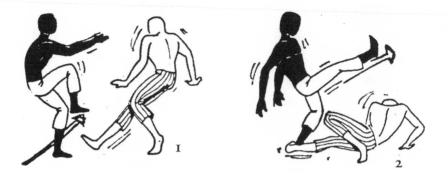

3. NEGATIVA DERRUBANDO

Our old acquaintance the *negativa* can be used not only as a means of movement on the floor but also in a takedown. A good example of this can be seen in the last movements of some of Bimba's Sequences (Third, Seventh and Eighth) where we see one partner attack with a *benção* and the other respond by going into a *negativa* and setting his foot behind the heel of the support leg of the attacker (notice that as Striped goes into a *negativa*, he conveniently dodges Plain's kick).

From that position, the person on the ground would pull his foot and leg in (as we saw when studying the *negativa*) and finish in a standing position while his partner falls.

In the diagrams we see the player going into the *negativa derrubando* from the basic *ginga*. In the diagram, Plain's *benção* has been frozen in midair for demonstration purposes. However, it should never be hanging in the air as seen in the diagram, but should be completed from start to finish as quickly as possible.

Exercises:

a) The best exercises for this takedown are in Bimba's Sequences. Work on trying to be quick enough to position yourself for the sweep while your partner's kicking leg is still in the air. The person kicking should concentrate on completing the kick, and should try to forget that he knows his partner is coming in for the takedown.

4. NEGATIVA WITH A TESOURA

Using forward momentum, the capoeirista goes into a *tesoura* and traps the leg of his opponent. The torque generated by Plain twisting his hip will knock "Striped" down (diagram 3).

Exercises:

a) *Ginga* in front of someone who is standing still in the *ginga* stance; then enter into the *negativa* and trap your opponent's leg with the *tesoura* (ten times each leg).

b) Both partners ginga. One steps into a *benção* while the other steps in with a *negativa tesoura* and traps his opponent's leg (ten times each leg).

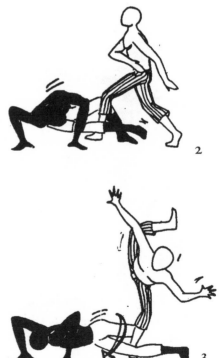

5. ARRASTÃO

We already saw this movement in Bimba's Fourth Sequence. The diagram shows in detail the impact of the shoulder against the top of the hip as both hands pull from behind the knee.

This movement is frequently used to defend against a punch or an attack with a club. It is most effective in a game situation when coupled with the element of surprise. It is common for the person who is being taken down to grab at his opponent's back. In that case, the person executing the movement should stand up, forcing his opponent's knees up and causing an ugly fall.

Exercises:

a) Go into the *arrastão* on a person who is stationary (ten times each leg).

b) *Ginga* in front of a stationary person; go into the *arrastão* (ten times each leg).

6. BOCA DE CALÇA

In spite of seeming rather naive, this move works wonderfully when applied quickly and shrewdly. It is very often used by *malandros* at the start of a fight.

In a game situation, when used from the *cocorinha* against a spinning kick (an *armada*, for example), the *boca de calça* is applied against only one leg (the support leg). Note that (as the name, which means pant hem, indicates) the person executing the move grabs the hem of the pants of the person he is trying to knock down.

Exercises:

Stand in a relaxed and casual manner in front of and close to your partner, who should be standing still. Bend down to grab both pant hems.

7. BOCA-DE-CALÇA DE COSTAS
(Baianada)

A now-classic *malandragem* move used to initiate fights when one has an opponent directly behind him. The diagram shows the *boca de calça* as it is being applied. The capoeirista jumps back at the same time that he bends down to grab the ankles, or the *boca de calça,* of the opponent. The resulting fall is very dangerous.

Exercises:

Practice coming in to execute this movement on a training partner who is standing. Beginning from a relaxed and casual position, jump back and reach down quickly and decisively (ten times each leg).

8. CRUZ
(Cruz de Carreira; Cruz de Encruzilhada)

When you are attacked by a *benção* or a similar kick, you can *esquiva* and take down your opponent with the *cruz*. Depending on the position of the person being attacked, he will *esquiva* to the inside or to the outside; using either of those two *esquivas* the capoeirista can enter and take down the opponent.

It is not easy to learn to come in and execute the *cruz*, but after some practice you will master it.

Exercises:

a) Both players ginga; one does the *benção*, and the other responds with the *cruz* (ten times each leg).

9. BANDA POR DENTRO

This is used if you are attacked by a *martelo* or a similar kick. As we can see in the diagram, the player on the right steps in with his right leg as he prepares to throw a *martelo* with his left leg. The other player astutely anticipates the attack; instead of backing up, he swiftly steps in with his right leg behind his left leg. When he is about to be attacked, he is already in a position to use his left leg to violently pull his opponent's right leg from under him while he pushes him in the chest or the chin (diagram 4).

Exercises:

a) Practice entering into the *banda por dentro* with your partner standing still (ten times).

b) Both partners *ginga*; one enters into a *martelo,* and the other responds with a *banda por dentro* (ten times each leg).

1

2

3

4

10. BANDA DE COSTA

In this takedown, the player thrusts forward, lands on one foot and executes the *banda,* all in one swift movement. It is most effective when both legs of the opponent are swept from under him, but that is quite difficult to do unless your opponent happens to be very naive. This is frequently used against an *armada* or a *queixada,* or during an unexpected moment in a game.

Exercises:

a) Step in to execute the *banda* on your partner while he is standing still (ten times each leg).

b) *Ginga* in front of your partner as he stands still, and come in for the *banda de costas* (ten times each leg).

c) Both partners *ginga;* one does a *giro* (spin; see Bimba's Fifth Sequence) while the other comes in to execute the *banda de costa* (ten times each leg).

I

2

11. AÇOITE-DE-BRAÇO

This is a movement geared more towards self-defense in case you are attacked by a person wielding a club or similar weapon, rather than in a game situation.

Exercises:

Execute the *entrada* as shown in the diagrams.

12. TESOURA

(Tesoura-de-costas, Tesoura Furada, Tesoura Voadora)

In the drawing we see that the player who is going to apply the *tesoura* approaches his opponent from afar (drawings 1 and 2). Only when he is near does he actually execute the takedown. The move works because of the torque generated by the body of the attacker, as seen in diagram 4. In practice, the *tesoura* can also be applied much closer.

Exercises:

  a) Come in from afar to execute the *tesoura* (ten times).
  b) Come in from up close (ten times).

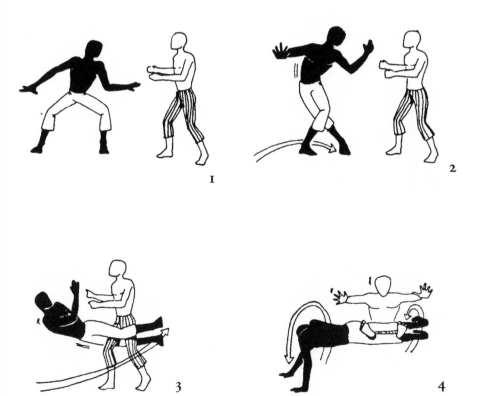

13. TESOURA-DE-FRENTE

It is common that, in the heat of the moment, as the players are exchanging kicks, one of the players, even for a split-second, foolishly leaves a leg vulnerable for the takedown. If the other player acts swiftly, he will be able to execute the *tesoura de frente.*

Exercises:

a) Execute the *entrada* on your partner as he stands still with one leg forward.

b) *Ginga* in front of your partner as he stands still and executes the *entrada* for the *tesoura-de-frente* (ten times each leg).

I

2

3

14. VINGATIVA

In diagrams 1, 2 and 3 we can see the *vingativa* as it is applied from the floor. Most likely, Striped tried to attack Plain, while Plain was on the floor, with a kick or a *joelhada* (knee-blow). But Plain was able to react quickly and to come up into the *vingativa,* placing his right leg behind his adversary's support leg and completing the takedown by using his leg and torso in a vise-like fashion to make his opponent lose his balance.

This takedown works very efficiently when the person executing it is standing up. In that case, he would proceed from a *ginga* position to the position shown in diagram 2.

Exercises:

a) Come in through the *negativa* on a person who is standing up (ten times each leg).

b) One person *gingas* standing up, and the other plays on the floor, changing directions in the *negativa.* The person standing tries to knee the person who is on the floor, and the latter tries to take down the attacker with a *vingativa* (ten times each side).

c) *Ginga* in front of a person who is standing; come in and execute the *vingativa* (ten times each side).

d) Two partners *ginga.* One executes the *giro,* and the other person comes in and executes the *vingativa* (ten times each side).

1

2

3

15. TOMBO-DE-LADEIRA

Capoeiristas often execute moves that temporarily leave them airborne and thus vulnerable to attack *(S-dobrado, Pulo-do-macaco, or compasso)*. In the *tombo-de-ladeira,* the opponent takes advantage of this split-second, rushes in under the person executing the airborne movement and stands up at the precise moment so as to knock him down. See *Cintura desprezada.*

There you have it: As a beginner, you now have enough material to begin developing your game. Of course, there are other, more advanced exercises for more advanced students, and students can learn some of these when my second and third books are translated into English.

OTHER KICKS AND MOVEMENTS

I want to stress once again the importance of the beginner frequenting the places where capoeira is practiced, even if it is not exactly what one had in mind, because things are rarely as we wish them to be—we sometimes have to learn to deal with what is at hand. Often we see in hindsight that those very critical observations we had once made about a particular place or situation were nothing other than excuses and rationalizations that permitted us to stay within a stagnant comfort zone.

At this point we would like to present you with a few movements now considered classical capoeira movements, well-known among a great number of capoeiristas.

The beginner should continue his training (although it should be remembered that the takedowns presented in the last pages should be practiced only after six months to a year of training), and can explore the following movements according to his curiosity and desire to learn new movements.

1. CHAPA-DE-FRENTE

This is the *Angoleiro's bênção.* Let's take this opportunity to explore the differences between the practitioners of *Angola* and *Regional.* Perhaps these differences are attributable to differences in class and education: The *Angoleiro* is the legitimate heir of the marginalized capoeira of the past.

Traditionally, the *Angoleiros* came from the economically least-favored and most-oppressed classes. The *Angoleiro* is accustomed

from a young age to confronting life's blows. The *Regional* practitioner, on the other hand, usually comes from the wealthy class. During his childhood, he usually had the protection of his parents, nannies, good schools, etc., which makes him more daring and to some extent more naive. He is not as accustomed to the hard, face-to-face battles with life and with the social structure. There is always something or someone ready to protect him and give him shelter.

Thus, in *Regional,* when the *bênção* is completed and the capoeirista continues to be on his feet, he simply recoils his foot after throwing the kick, without thinking about possible counterattacks. The *Angoleiro,* on the other hand, after completing the *bênção* (or in this case *chapa-de-frente*), seeks the protection of the floor against possible takedowns or counterattacks aimed at his face. The *Regional's bênção* aims at the chest, and tries to throw the opponent spectacularly out of the *roda.* The *Angoleiro's chapa-de-frente* does not seek such flashy results, but in real-life confrontations it aims for the groin and is very effective.

2. CRUZADO

(Pisão, Escorão)

This is another kick that "goes for broke."
It is similar to the *benção pulada* in that if
you are successful, great—but if not, you
are in trouble. If you miss, and your opponent is quick, he can come in for a take-

down, and your resulting fall will not be a pretty sight.

Along with the *martelo* and the *benção,* it is one of the few kicks
that can be and should be practiced on a sandbag.

3. S-DOBRADO

(Chapéu-de-Couro, Doublé-S)

This is a movement that is more difficult to describe (through pictures or words) than it is to execute.

The player goes down into a *corta-capim* (diagrams 1 and 2),
which is a type of *rasteira,* and at the end of the movement he thrusts

his foot (his left foot, in the drawing) up in the air while he shifts the weight of his body from his right hand to his left hand, and then thrusts his right leg up while supported by his left hand (diagram 4). In diagrams 5 and 6 we see the termination of the movement.

4. CHIBATA

(Rabo-de-Araia)

This is a very fast kick, similar to the *meia lua de compasso.* However, in the *chibata,* you do not put your hand on the ground for support. You make up for this lack of support with the speed with which you execute the kick. This kick is dangerous for the player on the receiving end because of the speed with which it is delivered, and it is dangerous for the person executing it in case he gets swept.

5. PONTEIRA

This is a quick and explosive frontal kick, very common in other martial arts. It uses the ball of the foot to strike the opponent, and leaves you vulnerable to *cruz* and *rasteira*.

6. VÔO-DO-MORCEGO

In the drawings we see the attacker gain momentum and leap into the *Vôo-do-morcego,* with both feet aimed at the face or the solar plexus of the opponent.

This kick can also be applied as a counterattack from the ground while in the *cocorinha* position. In that case, the capoeirista would go down into a *cocorinha* in order to dodge a kick (an *armada,* for example). Once the kick has passed, the player comes up directly from the *cocorinha* position into the position shown in diagram 2, and then extends both feet simultaneously (diagram 3). This kick can be practiced against a sand bag.

7. MACACO
(Pulo de Macaco)

This can be used as a way of moving within the *roda,* or as a blow when your opponent is behind you during a game.

In the drawings, the person executing the *macaco* changes his support hand, from his right (diagram 2) to his left (diagram 3). But the *macaco* can be executed without this change of hand. In that case, the person in the drawing would execute the *macaco* using the right hand only for support. Usually the kick is executed when the body is more contracted, and it is finalized with a double mule-kick at the end.

8. MEIA LUA PULADA
(Compasso, Meia Lua Solta)

This is a kick commonly used in Rio de Janeiro. The player proceeds as if about to go into a hand-spin (reach for the floor at a

diagonal with your hand going across your body), and completes the kick (diagrams 3 and 4). The kick is delivered with the heel. Some execute this kick without touching the ground with their hand (*meia lua solta*).

The classic counterattack for this movement is the *tombo-de-ladeira*.

9. COMPASSO

Similar to the previous kick; however, the trajectory of the leg follows a vertical plane (whereas, in the previous one, it followed a horizontal plane).

The *compasso* can be executed slowly, under control, in which case it would end in a *negativa* (diagram 4a), or it can be executed violently and with a lot of energy, in which case it would end almost standing up (diagram 4b).

Again, the classic counterattack here is the *tombo-de-ladeira*.

1

2

3

4a

4b

10. CHAPÉU-DE-COURO

The movement begins with a *martelo,* but then proceeds as shown above in diagrams 1, 2 and 3.

11. RABO-DE-ARRAIA

The capoeira terminology varies quite a bit from place to place. The same movement can have two different names, and sometimes the same name describes two different movements.

Among Brazilians, the *rabo-de-arraia* is perhaps the kick most associated with capoeira. Nonetheless, that terms refers to various quite different moves. Depending on the region, *rabo-de-arraia* can also be used to describe the kicks that in this book we call *meia lua de compasso* and *chibata.*

It seems, though, that the original *rabo-de-arraia* is the one shown in the diagram on the left, a movement typical of *Capoeira Angola.*

The kick is executed with the heel, and after completing it the player returns to position (diagram 1). It is not unusual for there to be contact with one heel and then another, as shown in the diagram, or to alternate both legs before returning to the original position (diagram 1).

12. ARMADA WITH MARTELO

The movement begins with an *armada* (diagrams 1, 2 and 3). Halfway through, the person executing this movement, taking advantage of the momentum, jumps while changing legs and goes into a *martelo* (diagram 4).

13. ARPÃO DE CABEÇA

This is a violent head-butt (we already saw this movement in Bimba's Sequences), wherein the person executing it uses the entire weight of his body.

The arms are crossed in front of the player's face in order to protect the face from a *joelhada* (knee-blow). The arms are opened on impact; this increases the power of the movement, which is aimed at the chest or the stomach of the adversary.

14. ESCORUMELO

The *cabeçada* (head-butt) is a move frequently used in capoeira: As long as there is an opening in the defenses, there exists the danger of a *cabeçada*. We have just explored the *arpão-de-cabeça*; here we see a *cabeçada*, which is even more vicious. In this movement the attacker comes up quickly, sliding his head along the chest of the opponent. The point of impact is usually the chin, the nose or the brow. Obviously this movement should never be carried out to completion in a game situation, since the consequences are quite serious.

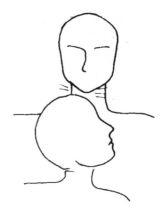

Although many don't realize it, capoeira also uses many hand blows. In *Angola* they are simply shown; that is, the players don't carry the blows out to completion, but stop just short of contact.[26]

This at times results in a veritable hand ballet of arms, hands and elbows—the so-called *jogo de mão*. In the *Regional*, which pays less attention to ritual and puts more emphasis on fight, the hand blows (the *galopante*, for example) are often carried out to completion.

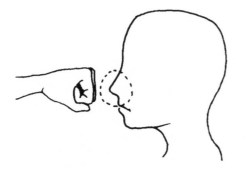

15. ASFIXIANTE

A brisk and direct punch aimed at the nose-mouth region.

---

26. In some of the hand movements in *Angola,* the players pretend to have a *navalha,* or knife.

16. GALOPANTE

A slap with your hand cupped—the entire outstretched arm and torso twist when executing this movement so as to generate more power. It is aimed at the base of the ear. This is also an extremely dangerous movement that can cause damage to the eardrum, and should never be carried out to completion in a *roda*.

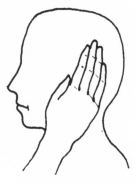

17. GODEME

This is a blow delivered by the knuckles of your fisted hand. A brisk and explosive movement is made with the forearm, and aimed at the brow.

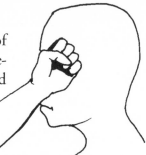

18. CUTELO

Any blow delivered using the outer edge of your stiffened hand.

19. CUTEVELADA

The elbows, due to the very movement of the arms in the *ginga,* are frequently used in capoeira.

20. DEDEIRA

A classic movement: The rigid index and middle fingers are used to poke the eye of the opponent. The element of surprise is key here. Obviously tremendously dangerous, and

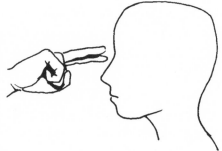

not to be carried out to completion (many times in the *roda* players will merely "show" this movement when there is an opening).

21. TELEFONE

A double slap to both ears simultaneously with hands cupped. Again, very dangerous and not to be carried out to completion in a *roda*.

> Capoeira,
> *Mandinga* of the slave
> yearning to be free.
> Its beginning has no method,
> Its end is inconceivable
> even to the wisest of mestres.
>
> (Mestre Pastinha)

THE LANGUAGE OF ANGOLA

apoeira Angola possesses its own language, which is often elusive to the non-initiated.

In the section entitled "O Jogo" ("The Game") we described briefly and superficially a situation where one of the players stands with his arms open, and the other player, after several *aús* and demonstrations of his flexibility and control, approaches his opponent, checks one of the legs of the player who is standing in order to prevent an unexpected kick, and slowly rises until they face each other with their arms outstretched and their hands touching. In this position, they take a few steps forward accompanying the rhythm of the beat, stop, and then take a few steps backwards.

This type of dialogue is one of the richest—and as amazing as it might seem, one of the most derided—aspects of *Capoeira Angola*.

PASSO-À-DOIS

There are many ways in which the individuals can come together in the *passo-à-dois*. Furthermore, they vary greatly according to the individuals involved and the situations that arise. A lot of *malícia* and a deep knowledge of the basics of the game are needed in order to be able to respond appropriately to whatever situation may arise, the reason being that, although these movements are often very ritualized, at other times they are more improvised and treacherous.

The *passo-à-dois* has different meanings, depending on the level at which one wants to understand it:

- Objectively, it is a way of resting and catching one's breath during the game, or a way of breaking the dynamics of the game of your opponent (as in basketball, when a coach asks for a time-out).

- From a martial-arts perspective, it strengthens the awareness of the player, who is required to approach an opponent from whom he does not know what to expect. Situations preceding actual fights in bars, on the street, etc., many times have this characteristic.

- From a philosophical perspective, the *passo-à-dois* teaches us that when someone is called to interact (in a new job or romance, or even buying or selling a car), that person should go in a very relaxed and self-confident way, but always keep an eye on his opponent to prevent any treachery. We also see that the most dangerous moments in any transaction are when you make the first contact or when you end the transaction and the partners are separating.

All of these levels of knowledge and experience are present in *Angola's* ritualistic movements, but few people really understand what is going on.

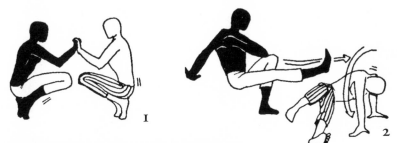

CHAMADA DE COCORINHA

Two players, while in the *cocorinha* position with both hands touching, move sideways with several small hops; one of the players breaks these successive hops with a *chapa de frente,* but the other player, just in the nick of time, manages to escape in the *negativa* and *rolê.*

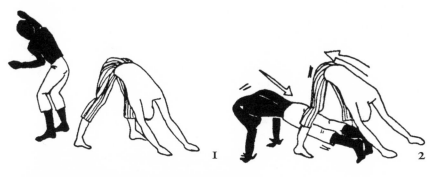

PASSAGEM DE TESOURAS

In the *passagem de tesouras,* one of the players slides underneath the open legs of his opponent. It is not unusual for the person sliding to attempt to strike his opponent with his heel (a *calcanheira*), or to execute a *boca de calça.*

SAÍDA PARA O JOGO

The entrance of the player into the *roda* from the foot of the *berimbau* and the *reverencia*—both of which were briefly described previously—are also part of the *Angola* vocabulary, and show the subtleties and the sophistication of the player.

VOLTA DO MUNDO

It is not unusual for one of the players to suddenly interrupt the game and to start walking or jogging around the *roda*. The other accompanies him in the *volta ao mundo* without knowing what will come next—perhaps a sudden kick, or an invitation to return to the foot of the *berimbau* and start the game anew.

QUEDA DE RINS

Literally, kidney *(rin)* fall *(queda)*, so named because in this movement the capoeirista's weight is balanced on his elbow, which in turn is placed near the kidney area. Both arms serve as support while the legs hang outstretched in the air.

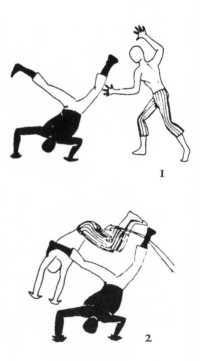

In the drawing, one of the players in the *queda de rins* invites the other to jump through his outstretched legs.

In short, *Capoeira Angola* is very rich in the kind of situations we have just described, in which both players are brought together to interact in ritualized ways. In the sequel to this book we intend to go into further detail on the subject matter.

138

FINAL WORDS

We have arrived at the end of our introductory exploration. The reader would do well to remember that the reality of the game is not simply the sum of the kicks, training methods and sequences shown here. Within the game, a player creates unique situations in which it is possible to release this or that kick or to proceed in this or that manner.

As your game develops further you will become aware that capoeira is not based on attack, but rather on *esquivas,* coming in under a kick and counterattacking or taking down the opponent.

Later—years later—the capoeirista gets the urge to enrich his or her game with aspects that have nothing to do with techniques or kicks but rather with the ritual of the game. There comes the urge to learn the aspects of *Angola* that we have just finished exploring. If this does not happen, the player can paint himself into a corner, and the game of capoeira can turn into a physical dispute, dull and frustrating.

We would hope that the final objective of showing the above kicks and exercises wouldn't be to have them repeated mechanically as illustrated in this book. The final objective is to prepare the capoeirista to react to diverse circumstances, improvising according to the situation and the moment at hand and, in a wider sense, learning how to look and interact in life in a way suggested by capoeira.

The philosophy and roots of capoeira come from the experience and knowledge of generations of players—how they played in the *roda* and how they played the game of life. The many kicks in this book are actually the result of improvisations that were successful in the past, and consequently became widely used, leading in time to the perfection of the movements, until they finally became considered traditional, classical kicks.

The moves and kicks shown here are like the letters of the alphabet: The exercises will teach the beginner to read and write. I hope that the reader eventually writes his or her own story, and plays the game in his or her very own way.

Nestor Capoeira

FINAL WORDS
TO THE ENGLISH EDITION

Since I first started teaching capoeira abroad in 1971 and, later on, when this *Little Book* was published in Brazil, I have always looked forward to an English version of my books.

But this is not easy. Capoeira is only beginning to spread its wings outside of Brazil, and few people have the insight to recognize that it is something that will become popular throughout the world in the next ten or twenty years. This means that, for the time being, publishing a book on capoeira is not attractive if you are looking for an immediate monetary return on your investment.

At the same time, I was afraid that the translation of the book would take away the flavor of its original version. Although I have lived for two years in the United States and five in Europe, I did not feel that my English was up to the task. I was lucky to meet Alex Ladd, who not only translated the book but also pinpointed special angles that would have to be further developed so that a reader from another culture could grasp meanings that are specific to Brazil.

I am very pleased with this final version. I hope that through it our *camaradas* from North America, England and other English-speaking countries will be able to share in the knowledge that has been passed down to us through generations of capoeira players.

Nestor Capoeira
Odenese, Denmark
November, 1994

GLOSSARY OF BASIC CAPOEIRA TERMS

(Compiled by A. Ladd)

Angola: *(See capoeira Angola)*

Arame: Literally 'wire.' An *arame* is attached to both extremeties of the *verga* (wooden bow) to create the berimbau. The *arame* is usually extracted from inside the inner rim of an old tire. Previously, animal entrails were used.

Atabaque: The drum used in capoeira *rodas*. Similar to the conga drum.

Baqueta: A wooden stick approximately 12 inches long used to strike the berimbau wire and thus create sound.

Berimbau: A bow-like percussive instrument which dictates the tempo of the music and consequently the tempo of the capoeira game. Commonly three types of berimbaus are present in the roda, the *gunga*, the *medio* and the *viola* or *violinha* (see those entries for more information). Mestre Bimba, however, opted for only one berimbau in the roda.

Cabaça: A gourd. To form the berimbau, the *cabaça* is dried out and hollowed. The *cabaça* is attached to the *verga* (wooden bow) and *arame* (wire) by way of a string ring to form a berimbau. The *cabaça* is the pecussive box which resonates the sound caused by striking the *arame* with the *baqueta* (small stick).

Capoeira Angola: With the advent of Mestre Bimba's *capoeira Regional* in the 1930s, the traditional capoeira became known as *capoeira Angola*. Generally performed to a slower rhythm, and movements are closer to the ground than in *Regional*. Games usually last longer and a premium is placed on the bodily dialog, the aesthetic qualities of the game and the *malandragem* (see entry for more information).

Capoeira Regional: A capoeira style created in Bahia in the1930s by Mestre Bimba (Manoel dos Reis Machado). Bimba modified many of the existing kicks in the traditional capoeira to create a more upright and aggressive style. *Regional* is usually practiced to a much quicker beat than Angola, usually to one of the several berimbau rhythms created by Bimba. Today the *Regional* style originally practiced by Bimba and his pupils is rarely seen. Instead there is a hybrid that could be called *Regional/Senzala* (see *Senzala* for more information).

Chulas: Can be used to denote chants in general, or a medium length chant, shorter than a *ladainha* but longer than a *corrido*.

Cintura desprezada: Literally 'scorned hips.' A sequence of four acrobatic exercises created by Mestre Bimba wherein the capoeirista learns to always fall on his feet.

Corpo fechado: Literally 'closed body.' A person who, through specific magic rituals, supposedly attains almost complete invulnerability in the face of various weapons.

Corridos: One or two verse songs sung by the "soloist" and answered by the chorus. The shortest among the three most common types of songs in the capoeira roda. *Corridos* are common in both capoeira *Angola* and *Regional.* The other two are the *ladainha* and the *quadras* (see those entries for more information).

Fundamentos: Literally 'basis' or 'origins.' Used to describe the philosophical roots of capoeira.

Gunga: The bass berimbau. When played in unison with the berimbau *medio* and the *violinha*, it is responsible for keeping the rhythm.

It normally plays the basic theme of a certain beat with very little variation. A particularly deep sounding *gunga* is also referred to as a *berra boi* ('bellowing ox' in Portuguese).

Jogo: Literally 'game' in Portuguese. Used to denote the activity inside the roda (circle). The verb is to *jogar* capoeira, i.e. to play capoeira.

Ladainha: The soulful songs that typically mark the begining of a roda or a game. The *ladainhas* are not call and response but rather are sung by a soloist, usually crouched at the foot of the berimbau. However, at the end of the *ladainha* the singer will go into a *canto de entrada,* where he praises capoeira mestres, places, or famous capoeiristas, and then the chorus responds in acknowledgement by repeating what was just praised. For example, the soloist will sing *Yê, viva Pastinha* (*Yê,* long live Pastinha). The chorus will then respond *Ê, viva Pastinha, camará.*

The *ladainhas* are typical of capoeira Angola. Mestre Bimba would not sing *ladainhas* in his rodas. instead he would sing *quadras* and *corridos* (see those entries for more information).

Malandro: A rogue or hustler. The *malandro* is a fixture in capoeira lore and in Brazilian popular culture in general. *Malandragem* is a tricky or deceitful act.

Mandinga: Magic or sorcery. The word implies a basic understanding of the forces of nature, and that the person in question knows how to use them by means of rituals involving magic. A *mandingueiro* is one well versed in *mandinga.*

Medio: Also known simply as berimbau or *berimbau de centro.* It plays the role similar to the rhythm guitar when played together with the *gunga* and the *violinha.* It typically plays the basic theme of a certain beat, then a basic variation on that theme, then it returns to the basic theme and so on.

Mestre: A capoeira master. Nowadays, many schools grant that title to students who have completed certain requirements. Traditionally, however, the title is conferred by capoeiristas themselves and the public at large to those who have proven themselves over many years (usually no less than ten) as both capoeiristas and teachers.

Pandeiro: The Brazilian tambourine.

Passo-à-dois: Literally, 'stepping in unison' in Portuguese. A ritualized movement typical of capoeira Angola. The *passo-à-dois* is initiated by one of the players inside the capoeira *roda* by stopping suddenly in the middle of a game and raising one arm or both arms. The other player then has to come and meet him in one of several prescribed manners, then together they take three steps forward, then three steps backwards and then cautiously resume the game.

Patúa: A magic amulet usually worn around the neck as protection against evil and injury.

Quadras: Four verse songs sung by the "soloist" and answered by the chorus. Typical of Mestre Bimba and capoeira *Regional*.

Rasteira: A sweep. One of the trademark capoeira moves.

Regional: *(see capoeira Regional)*

Roda: Literally means 'wheel' in Portuguese. This is the circle in which capoeira takes place. The roda is usually made up of other capoeiristas or bystanders standing or sitting in a circle.

Senzala: A capoeira group formed in Rio de Janeiro in the mid 1960s by a group of young capoeiristas. The Senzala group was responsible for adding several new warm up and teaching techniques. They also built on the work of Manoel dos Reis Machado (Mestre Bimba) and modified existing kicks and movements.

Verga: A stick usually about four to five feet tall which is used to form the berimbau bow. The *verga* is usually made from a Brazilian wood known as *biriba*. *Vergas* can also be made of other flexible woods or bamboo. A wire (usually removed from the inside rim of a tire) is attached to both extremities and a gourd (*cabaça*) is attached to the bottom to serve as a resonating box.

Vintém: An old coin used in Brazil and Portugal. Also used to denote the object used by the berimbau player to evoke different sounds from the berimbau. A *vintém* can be a heavy coin, a washer or a stone. By pressing the *vintém* hard against the *arame* (wire), you can produce a higher note, and by simply resting it against the wire you create a muffled sound. Not using the *vintém* at all produces the low note. The *vintém* can also be called a *dobrão*.

Viola (violinha): The berimbau that has the highest pitch; it has the most freedom to syncopate or to improvise when combined with other berimbaus (the *gunga* and the *medio*). The role that it plays is equivalent to that of the solos of a lead guitar.

APPENDIX: CAPOEIRA TRENDS

UPDATING THE LITTLE CAPOEIRA BOOK

The value of *The Little Capoeira Book* is its simplicity and its panoramic bird's-eye view of the capoeira scenery: the history, the music, the ritual, the philosophy, and a synthesized teaching method for beginners.

It's like the map of a city. It can help you find your way around.

But on the other hand, it lacks a lot of "deeper," more detailed information. Not to mention that in order to know a city (or to know capoeira) one must personally live there and get involved.

The Little Capoeira Book was published in 1995 and revised in 2002, after selling some 20,000 copies. Both North Atlantic Books and I felt it was time for some "updating."

Since my second book appeared in English in 2002—*Capoeira: Roots of the Dance-Fight-Game*—much more historical material is now available to the interested reader. I decided to take this reprinting opportunity to include in *The Little Capoeira Book* a report on the speeches and discussions of a very important capoeira meeting in 1984. Although the meeting occurred many years ago now, it and a follow-up conference in 1990 were seminal in defining modern capoeira. The ideas, questions, and answers of different well-known capoeira *mestres* give us insight into some of the central issues of capoeira today. Also, due to the later growth of capoeira, those years were the only ones in which it would ever be possible to meaningfully gather the majority of high-level players—the leaders of the capoeira world—together in one place.

The topics addressed at those conferences are explored fully in my other two books, but I wanted to summarize some of them for the revised edition of *The Little Capoeira Book* so that it remains a relevant introduction for people who may never read another book on the subject.

My second book, *Capoeira: Roots of the Dance-Fight-Game,* contains interviews with scholars who specialize in Afro-Brazilian culture and also played capoeira when younger; points of view of various knowledgeable mestres; and testimonies of players who knew and were closely associated with Mestre Pastinha, Mestre Bimba, and many others who are no longer with us. That book goes deeply into capoeira's philosophy—*malícia*—comparing it with the Western way of thinking as well as the Eastern way of being.

Capoeira: Roots of the Dance-Fight-Game tries to capture capoeira's modern era, with its different groups and styles. I discuss how they relate to each other using different strategies and "approaches" in order to lead or to have greater influence on the capoeira scene as a whole. I also introduce a theme of special interest for the English-speaking player: the role to be played in the 2000s by European and North American capoeiristas. Finally, I include a few exercises and training routines for advanced players.

What specifically connects my first and second books is the inclusion of this new Appendix in *The Little Capoeira Book*. It rounds out the "map" and takes the reader into the present manifestation of capoeira. This summary of the 1984 conference, together with my notes from the 1990 conference in *Capoeira: Roots of the Dance-Fight-Game,* constitute important background material for the modern capoeirista. I'm happy to finally make this material available in English.

In order to understand the deeper concerns and details of specific issues presented in the Appendix and my later books, it is necessary to keep in mind the "panorama" given in *The Little Capoeira Book.*

Let's consider some examples:

- We must keep in mind what historical period we are talking about. Events that happened in the slavery period (up to the end of the 1800s) occur in a very specific context, and we should not confuse ourselves thinking they happened in the early 1900s, when it is almost the "academy period" with Mestres Pastinha and Bimba.

- We must have in mind what town are we talking about. For example, since around 1850, capoeira in Rio was "mixed" in its association with color of skin and social class. Military men, street characters, and others used capoeira for their own ends. The black "roots" weren't as important to them. This is completely different from what happened in Salvador, where capoeira was practiced exclusively by the blacks and mulattos of the underprivileged economic classes until the 1930s, when Bimba opened his Regional academy.

- We must know what style we are talking about, and know that a certain style can maintain its name although deep changes occur in it. For example, the Capoeira Angola practiced by different mestres until 1950/1960 is very different from the contemporary Angola. The movements are similar and so is the "berimbau orchestra." But it is as if the "shell," the outside and visible part, was maintained while the inside was modified. The Capoeira Angola pre-1960 was very free in the way it was taught and learned. It was also very free in the way it looked at the world, with a cosmos-vision that came from the *candomblé* religion and a street-smart roguish and relaxed approach to life (the art of *malícia*). Today's Angola teaching and learning are completely systematic (doing a movement "this" way is "right," doing it "that" way is "wrong"). And today's Angola "speech" is very dogmatic. Pupils learn it in the academy and repeat it as if they were parrots (it is overly serious, "politically correct black speech," having lost its fun and freedom).

A similar line of thought could be developed in regard to Capoeira Regional and more specifically to the groups that play the more recent Regional-Senzala style. Their teaching method is extremely effective but too rigid. It does not allow for creativity and improvisation, although it enables you to do a beautiful and impressive performance. And many of the players are always talking about "my work" and what they have "done for capoeira." (It seems that capoeira has done nothing for them.) They are extremely arrogant (they've lost the flexibility and the slyness), but nonetheless they are always saying "how important it is to be humble" (which in fact, similar to "work," was never a capoeira "quality"). They engage themselves in big campaigns sponsored by the government or by television, doing the "we are going to save the world" thing. They are always trying to look and dress like a serious Physical Education teacher at an expensive university, or some middle-class playboy who practices a "deadly martial art."

Despite the stereotyped and overly critical pictures that I give, the truth is that the "world vision" and "way of relating to life" of the majority of contemporary players, no matter the style, is narrower than before. But, luckily, inside the vast mediocre majority there are some exceptional human beings that also happen to be capoeira mestres.

And if I do this (slightly unfair and stereotyped) criticism of mestres who, notwithstanding what I think or say, do have something to give, it is in the hope that we avoid the worst-case scenarios and that we seek and carry on something positive and legitimate, with a lot of swing, *malícia,* and joy of living.

THE CONFERENCES AND DEBATES OF THE 1984 NATIONAL MEETING OF THE ART OF CAPOEIRA

The First National Meeting of the Art of Capoeira in 1984, and the second conference held in 1990, both in Rio de Janeiro, were attended by most of the main young and old mestres of that period. Many of them are presently world-renowned mestres in the beginning of the twenty-first century. Reading about their doubts and questions in 1984 and comparing them with the 1990 discussions gives us a very instructive picture of the radical changes capoeira went through at that time. These changes are part of the capoeira that is being practiced in the 2000s. As mentioned, I think that providing this historical background to English players/readers will be useful in understanding both capoeira's past and present.

One of the main changes that we can already foresee in the 1984 meeting is the rebirth or "return" of Capoeira Angola, which was eclipsed by the Regional style of Mestre Bimba beginning in the 1930s and the later advent of the Senzala group in Rio (strongly influenced by Bimba's Regional). We have already talked about this subject in the chapter "Capoeira Nowadays—the 1990s," and I examine in my later books why and how this "rebirth of Angola" happened.

In the 1984 meeting we can feel, for the first time since the 1930s, the importance given by the young mestres of the Regional-Senzala generation (around 30 to 40 years old in 1984) to the mestres of the *velha guarda da angola"* from Salvador. We should not forget that at that moment (1984) these old mestres were completely eclipsed by the new generation of Regional-Senzala players, up to a point where it was impossible for them to make a living from capoeira. The *"velha guarda"* had no more pupils and its members were never the center of attention in capoeira events. The 1984 meeting changed this picture.

We also see issues arising such as "racism in capoeira," "women in capoeira," "how science can help but should not overwhelm the art of capoeira," "distortion and loss of roots," etc., that had not been widely discussed before. A cycle had been completed (approximately 1965 to 1985) when the Regional-Senzala style was hegemonic and undisputed, and competitive "sport capoeira" was the only one on the day's agenda.

A new cycle was beginning, and looking back we can see that the 1984 meeting, as reinforced by the 1990 meeting, was the first visible sign of what was going on.

I believe that this cycle that began in 1984 is now, in the first years of the new millennium, coming to its end.

Most people don't see it because things don't usually end abruptly with something "new and different" starting at a precise moment and place. The characteristics of the old cycle continue to exist together (in harmony or in antagonism) with the fresh characteristics of the new cycle.

In my opinion, we can say that a new cycle started around 2000.

Some of the main characteristics of the 1985–2000 cycle included "capoeira as art," "capoeira as a practical philosophy of life," "capoeira as a way of living life," and from a more objective point of view, "the rebirth or return of Capoeira Angola." This cycle contrasted with the 1965–1985 cycle centered on "competitive sport capoeira," "championships and Capoeira Federations," and "uniform, hierarchic systems" (the colored ropes tied around the waist).

One of the main characteristics of the "new cycle" that began around 2000 is the role played by new "gringo" teachers and mestres from Europe and the USA (and later on, from other areas).

Already we see some non-Brazilian capoeira teachers giving classes. Most of them are "under" the supervision of a Brazilian mestre. But there are already a few who have their own independent group, and some of them are doing a good job.

Americans and Europeans have a very different mentality from Brazilians. When we have more non-Brazilian mestres in the near future, the capoeira scene is going to change.

The "external" and visible part of capoeira—the "shell" that includes the movements, the music, the *roda*—will probably continue in a similar way. But the mentality, the ideology, the different strategies of the power games between different areas, will radically change.

Capoeira changed similarly around 1965 when the center of happenings was no longer Salvador but Salvador/Rio/São Paulo.

Capoeira changed again around 1985 with the return of Capoeira Angola.

Capoeira Angola pre-1960 is deeply different (in the mentality, the ideology, the different strategies of the power games) from Capoeira Angola after 1985, although the "shell" is similar.

Eric Hobsbawn examines the "brief twentieth-century history" in one of his books and says something like: "the speculations of historians and other 'prophets' after World War II were shown to be spectacularly wrong, and it is possible that this performance has gotten even worse."

Warned by Hobsbawn, I won't play the role of the prophet in regard to this new capoeira cycle that I say began in 2000. But I cannot restrain myself from saying that I imagine the new changes will have to do with 1) "culture" as the Europeans understand it, i.e., a deeper interest in history, etc., and 2) "business and technology" as the Americans understand it (more use of videos, Internet, etc.).

Probably the English-speaking reader knows more than I about these last issues and could better predict what these new contributions might be. I believe that, as always, capoeira will gain something and lose something.

Perhaps with the new "cultural" contribution, including a deeper interest in history and research into the "roots," my own work will be more valued.

But probably those who value this path will look down at players who do not have access to orthodox Western education. The shitty "academic talk" will try to make itself more important than the body-dialogue (the Game) itself. And probably I will be one of the main "shit-talkers," a dinosaur who knew Mestres Pastinha and Bimba and who was part of the genesis of the Senzala group in the 1960s.

As for business and technology, we will probably see "experts" in these areas acquiring great importance in the capoeira world notwithstanding the fact that they might be poor players and know very little about the game.

People will say that "capoeira is losing its roots," that "distortions are being introduced in capoeira," and, up to a certain point, they will be right.

This is nothing new.

But capoeira has its own ways, regardless of what you or I want or like. It still remains up to us—you and me, and especially the non-Brazilian capoeirista—to try to ensure that regardless of "new contributions" we maintain the positive and traditional characteristics of this game that we love and are so attached to.

THE PIONEER MEETINGS OF 1968 AND 1969

To set the stage for discussion of the 1984 meeting and its follow-up in 1990, I'd like to expand the historical context a bit more. Today we have international capoeira meetings and workshops with a great number of qualified mestres and teachers from Brazil and all over the world. In fact, due to the great number of teachers (some say there are 25,000 in Brazil and around 1,000 abroad in the year 2000), it is no longer possible to have a meeting representing the whole of the capoeira community. And even if that could be done, there would be so many people that person-to-person relationship, which is basic to capoeira, would be impossible.

But it has not always been like that. In 1968 and 1969 we had the first "national" meeting including the majority of capoeira teachers and mestres throughout Brazil. For a brief period in capoeira history, not only was it possible to all sit down together, but we finally were able to actually do so.

As we have seen, around 1970 capoeira was practiced only in the state of Bahia (and mostly in its capital city, Salvador) and in Brazil's two largest cities, Rio de Janeiro and São Paulo, where capoeira had migrated some ten or twenty years before. Other big towns, such as Belo Horizonte, capital of the rich state of Minas Gerais, were still in the "heroic" and romantic period—with the appearance and disappearance of small, "non-professional" groups—that historically is often present before capoeira definitively establishes itself somewhere.

Around 1970, these other big towns generally had only one incipient small group of ten or twenty young capoeira players. These small groups trained irregularly, without the leadership of an experienced teacher. Participants were mostly from the upper middle class, similar to capoeiristas of Bimba's Regional style in Salvador and the successful Senzala group in Rio. This is in contrast to the traditional capoeira player (from Salvador) who belonged to the lower economic classes deeply rooted in Afro-Brazilian culture.

Thus when we say that in 1968 and '69 the first national meeting with all of Brazil's mestres rocked the capoeira world, we're talking about 100 teachers and mestres from Salvador (and a few other towns from the state of Bahia), Rio, and São Paulo. This is very different from the early 2000s, when there are so many capoeira players around the world and few delve deeply into the roots. However, because what was discussed here set the stage for the capoeira that developed, I think it is important to introduce this history to modern capoeira players, especially non-Brazilians.

These first two meetings were organized by a player called Dick Fersen, who disappeared from the capoeira scene some years later. I never saw or heard about him again; it was as if he vanished into thin air.

He managed to get the Brazilian Military Air Force to sponsor the events. The Air Force furnished the plane tickets, accommodations at one of their facilities on the outskirts of Rio, as well as a big auditorium equipped with loudspeakers and microphones. This was something very "big" for Brazilian standards of those times.

I (a young player of twenty-few years of age who had just attained Senzala's highest degree, the coveted "red-rope") was present and active in these pioneer meetings, together with my young Senzala colleagues, capoeiristas from Rio's outskirts, capoeiristas from the mega-city of São Paulo, and young and old capoeiristas from Bahia.

It must sound bizarre to have the military sponsoring capoeira in the end of the 1960s. This was during the military dictatorship period (1964–1984), when capoeira still suffered a lot of prejudice as "something done by bandits and street-smarts," "something done by negroes," "something from the lower classes."

But there is a historical association that explains this bizarre military support. If we say that capoeira from Bahia had a subtle link with Afro-Brazilian religion, it is also fair to say that Rio's capoeira had a subtle link with the military. Let's look at some examples over the last 200 years:

- Already in the early 1800s there were capoeira players in Rio that fled police persecution by enlisting in the *Guarda Nacional*, the official "armed fist" of the town and country rich aristocracy.

- In 1865, during the war against Paraguay, batallions composed of capoeiristas "enlisted" by force in the streets or in the prisons specialized in invading and conquering enemy trenches and enemy ships using mostly "white weapons" (bayonets, machetes, swords, etc.). The fearsome bloody deeds of these batallions were such that among the military the myth was born that "the capoeirista is the *Brazilian Warrior.*" It's a bizarre paradox if we keep in mind that the capoeiristas were black slaves or black free men who had no place in society, or they were lawless scoundrels, rogues, bandits, and street-smarts persecuted by the police.

- In the end of the 1800s, Rio's Chief of Police Ludgero da Silva realized that it was impossible to eradicate the capoeira *maltas* (gangs) that infested Rio's streets, and that it also was impossible to put in jail dangerous capoeiristas who worked as bodyguards or "hit men" for powerful politicians. He chose to establish a relationship that on one hand persecuted the capoeiristas but on the other hand absorbed many of them into his own ranks.

- In the beginning of the 1900s, when capoeira was already officially outlawed (1892–1934)—despite the fact that the heavy police persecution had practically extinguished capoeira in Rio as well as Recife—it was in small, secluded military circles in Rio that the first capoeira manuals were published for the exclusive consumption of the brothers-in-arms.

- Later on, in the early 1930s, Sinhozinho (a military officer who was the fighting instructor of the feared *Polícia Especial* of Dictator Vargas) successfully established his capoeira academies in Rio, first in the busy town-center and later in the rich Ipanema Beach district.

- Much later, around 1960, it was a navy officer specialized in Physical Education, Lamartine Pereira da Costa, who published the first successful book on "modern and sport capoeira"—*Capoeira sem Mestre.* That book continued to sell very well up to the 1980s.

These are only a few elements of the bizarre "love affair" between the outlawed and persecuted capoeira and the military and the police in Rio de Janeiro. Thus it is understandable that somewhere in the high ranks of the 1960s Brazilian Air Force there remained officers influenced not only by the myth created around capoeira, but its 200-year-old presence within the military.

And it was one of these top-brass officers that Dick Fersen managed to contact and convince of the importance of holding this revolutionary meeting that presumably would set capoeira on a new path as the legitimate "Brazilian Martial Art."

The agendas of the 1968 and '69 meetings were directed toward creating one (and only one throughout all Brazil) "capoeira uniform" (white trousers, white t-shirt, and white tennis shoes), one hierarchic system (ropes of different colors tied around the waist, similar to the belts worn in judo and karate), and one nomenclature for the movements and blows (which had and still have different names in Brazil's various regions as well as in capoeira's different styles).

It was planned that after these preliminary goals were achieved, the main issue would be taken up: we would create a National Capoeira Confederation under the watchful eyes of the government's National Sports Confederation, such as those already existing for soccer (Brazil's most popular sport), boxing, and many other "organized and disciplined" martial arts.

To those who know the capoeira world, it is needless to say that not even one of the preliminary goals (one uniform, graduation system, and nomenclature for all) was achieved.

There were a lot of unsuccessful discussions, power games, and clashes of egos.

To most (who wanted a "sportsmanlike," competitive, organized, and disciplined capoeira), it seemed that the 1968 and '69 pioneer meetings were a big failure. They might have said that capoeira and its capoeiristas were not mature and ready for the big step that would definitively take capoeira from its old roguish past toward what it should be: the true and only Brazilian Martial Art.

Many contemporary capoeiristas and mestres feel the same way nowadays.

But many others, myself included, have differing points of view. We see capoeira as something unique (not a sport, not a martial art) that has its own philosophy, ritual, and way of being. A part of Brazilian culture with its own specific message to deliver.

And in that sense, the pioneer meetings of 1968 and '69 were much more than a "success" or not. For the first time all those guys were together under the same roof, each one seeing the incredible "whole." All of us participated in the many *rodas* that happened throughout the event. Person-to-person contact between old mestres and young "revolutionary" teachers gave everyone new perspectives.

Everyone who was there was (unconsciously or consciously) rocked in his very soul.

Although this was not voiced at the moment, everyone somehow perceived that the old dream shared by Bimba, Pastinha, and so many others—a capoeira that would spread throughout Brazil and the world—was starting to become reality.

THE 1984 "CAPOEIRA ART" MEETING

Fifteen years later, in 1984, after the "unsuccessful" national meetings of 1968 and '69 sponsored by the Brazilian Air Force, the *Primeiro Encontro Nacional da Arte Capoeira* (First National Meeting of the Art of Capoeira) was held at the Circo Voador, a former circus modernized to become a fashionable dancing place and cultural center in Rio.

The meeting was organized by Camisa, a very young capoeirista who had trained with Mestre Bimba (in Salvador) and who had come to Rio with his older brother, the famous Camisa-Roxa. Camisa-Roxa was a respected friend of the Senzala "red-ropes," so Camisa entered the Senzala group in 1972 as a teenager. (Almost twenty years later, Camisa left Senzala and started his own group, Abada.)

Camisa was supported by Perfeito Fortuna, one of Circo Voador's managers, and also by a member of the INACEN (National Institute of Scenic Arts). The Senzala group helped to organize the conference, and I was asked to give a written report of the proceedings.

The meeting took place over a week with sixty-four players (including teachers and mestres) coming from eight different states: Bahia (led by Mestre Itapoã), São Paulo (with the well-known mestres Suassuna from Itabuna and Gato Preto from Salvador, both cities in Bahia), Brasília (Mestre Tabosa's group), Minas Gerais (Mestre Macaco's "Ginga" group from Belo Horizonte), Espírito Santo (led by Capixaba, one of Camisa's pupils, and Luis Paulo, a pupil of Peixinho, all from Senzala), Pernambuco (Mestre Mulatinho's—originally from Senzala—"Malês" group), Ceará (led by Canario and Paulão, Camisa's pupils, from Senzala), and Rio with Mestre Camisa's and Mestre Peixinho's group, both from Senzala. The Senzala group itself was represented, with all the "red-ropes," along with Mestre Martin's group and Mestre Corvo's group from the outskirts of Rio, and Moraes' Angola group, "Pelourinho."

Some of the *velha guarda* (old masters) from Salvador such as Valdemar da Paixão, Canjiquinha, João Pequeno, and Atenilo (the only one representing Salvador Regional style) were also present. There were a few capoeiristas and mestres who were teaching abroad (China, Paulo Siqueira, and Samara from Europe, and Acordeon from the USA).

Most of the capoeiristas present belonged to the Senzala group in Rio and in other states.

Some very young capoeiristas who attended became quite famous later on, such as Mão Branca who leads the "Capoeira Geraes"; Paulão, Boneco, and Paulinho Sabiá who left Senzala and created "Capoeira Brazil," etc.

There were no capoeira classes given by different teachers as is common in workshops abroad nowadays. Each afternoon there was a conference followed by questions and debates; at night a group from one of the states would present themselves, followed by a group from Rio. There were also many *rodas* happening all the time. So it was possible to see how capoeira was played in "faraway" places. We already see a great difference between this 1984 meeting (taking place in a well-known cultural center) and the '68 and '69 meetings (held in a military quarter on the outskirts of Rio). In 1968 and '69 there was an effort to "organize and discipline" capoeira, with a uniform, hierarchy, etc. In this 1984 meeting we already see another approach: "the Art of Capoeira."

In 1984 nothing was imposed. It was a meeting for exchanging experience and finding out what was happening with capoeira in Brazil and abroad. It was a real broadening of view.

But, on the other hand, there was also a "narrowing." In the 1968 and '69 meetings "all" teachers, mestres, and capoeira styles were represented. In the 1984 meeting most of the chosen sectors were from the Senzala group and from Bimba's Regional.

The following topics were on the agenda:

- "History of the Senzala Group" by Mestre Rafael Flores from Rio

- "Art and Science in Capoeira" by Mestre Ricardo "Macaco" Machado from Belo Horizonte
- "Women in Capoeira" by Marcia, Edna, Morena, and Luísa with the help of the women players from Rio's Senzala
- "Capoeira inside the (government) Federation" by Mestre João Mulatinho from Recife
- "Capoeira in the United States" by Mestre Bira "Acordeon," a graduate of Mestre Bimba who has taught in California since 1978
- "Loss of Roots and How to Preserve Capoeira": debate with Mestre Moraes
- "Capoeira in Bahia" by Mestre Cesar "Itapoã," a graduate of Mestre Bimba
- "A talk with the mestres of the *velha guarda*."

HISTORY OF THE SENZALA GROUP

The interest in the Senzala group can be explained by its great success in the 1970s and '80s. In 1984 Senzala had seventeen teachers (which was quite a lot for those times) of a very high technical playing level who were 30–40 years old and at the peak of their physical performance.

Initially they all taught in the same place. In the early 1970s they started teaching in different parts of Rio, and then expanding to the cities of Vitória and Fortaleza (something very rare at that time), and even to California and New York as well.

Senzala had a particularly interesting characteristic: it never had a mestre or a "chief."

The group started around 1964 with a bunch of young teenagers that trained by themselves. In 1984 some had been giving classes for more than fifteen years, each with his own group but all under the name "Senzala" (which is an old term for the slaves' quarters).

Rafael Flores is one of Senzala's founders. Although he left Rio and daily capoeira practice in 1980 to take care of his family's farm upon his father's death, Rafael says that Senzala lives deeply in his heart. It is a passionate love affair. He told conference participants some of the group's history.

I myself was a member of Senzala for more than twenty years (from 1968 to 1990, when I broke off to do my own thing), and I think I have a more critical point of view than Rafa's, which might come in handy as a counterpoint.

Rafael was born in Bahia. As a kid he saw an older cousin using capoeira during a fight in Salvador's elegant Rua do Chile and was very impressed. Later, his family moved to Rio but capoeira and its fascinating mystical aura never left his imagination.

At that time, around 1960, there were already a few good capoeira teachers in Rio. The most famous were the "Bonfim" Angola group (that still exists) and the (then) young mestre Artur Emidio from Itabuna (Bahia), who had come to town for several free-style fighting matches (with fighters from boxing, Brazilian jiu-jitsu, etc.). "Mestre Artur was already creating a school and tradition in the capoeira of Rio's outskirts," said Rafa. "But it was during a school holiday in Salvador that my brother Paulo and I took classes with Mestre Bimba, and my brother Nelson took classes with Mestre Pastinha."

This was the humble beginning of Senzala. "After one or two months of capoeira classes we returned to Rio and to school and started training on the terrace of the building we lived in, in the [upper middle class] quarter of Laranjeiras. Many of our young teenage friends and nearby neighbors would watch and even train with us, but I felt that none of them were deeply interested and in love with capoeira up to the point of really dedicating themselves to it."

The first one to arrive and definitively stay was Fernando "Gato."

This was in the early '60s, and different streets had their small groups of teenagers fighting one another. "At a gala fifteenth birthday party of a girlfriend, where teenagers wore suits and ties and quickly got drunk on the new drink *Cuba Libre*, Paulo Flores, my brother, had an argument and both groups of teenagers went out to the street. Gato, who we did not know, had a steel wire whip in his pocket—his basic equipment—together with Japanese spring jackknives."

The fight between the two youngsters started. "Paulo did the *ginga* from one side to the other.... Everybody was mesmerized: what the fuck was going on? He suddenly delivered a *benção* in his opponent's chest. His opponent was thrown backwards, bumped into a parked car, and came back. Paulo released a *rabo-de-arraia* that whistled in the air three inches away from the other boy's nose. There was a sudden silence. No one had ever seen anything similar. The fight ended that moment and Gato, very impressed, went to talk to Paulo and me, who told him about the trainings on the terrace. The following Monday Gato came to the training session and is still in Senzala today."

Later the group met another youngster called Claudio "Brasília" who was teaching capoeira to a friend nicknamed "Peixinho" in the garage of their building. The group got two new members. "Claudio Brasília stayed more than ten years in Senzala, until the 1970s, and then went off and became a very successful architect developing big projects such as the construction of universities in Africa, etc."

Peixinho was a quiet and non-competitive fellow who trained diligently. When his friend Claudio left in the '70s he already was one of Senzala's best players. Today, in the 2000s, Peixinho (who is well over 50) is Senzala's number-one player and one of Brazil's best.

His secret?

Hard training, a relaxed mind that refuses to engage in the power games and envious feelings that permeate the capoeira world, no drinking, no smoking, lots of fishing and surfing for pleasure and relaxation, and a sincere dedication to beautiful young ladies in their early twenties. Up to now, Mestre Peixinho never married and is one of the only "red-ropes" from the original group who doesn't have children.

"Shortly after," continues Rafael, "two young brats around 10 years old, nicknamed Garrincha and Sorriso, were 'recruited' and started to appear at the training sessions once in a while." This was the first contribution the *favelas* (slums) made to Senzala, because all the other youngsters were white upper-middle-class boys. Soon Gil "Velho" joined the group. He was Gato's brother, a teenager weighing almost 100 kg of solid muscles, incredibly agile and supple, with a broad-minded view of the world.

"And then when things were really starting to move, a problem came up: we had to leave the terrace where we trained. We were training our *bençãos* and *pisões* so hard on the terrace's walls that we cracked them."

Bad luck sometimes leads to good results. "Searching for a new place to train, we finally made contact with some of Rio's other capoeira spots. First with Valdo Santana, an older guy from Bahia who taught in Cinelândia in the very heart of downtown. Then we discovered a longshoremen's club by the docks were stevedores trained boxing and capoeira and did some weight-lifting. It was there I met and saw for the first time Artur Emidio," relates Rafael. "He was training his deadly and powerful *martelos* on the punching bag."

During these months of wandering around, training for a few weeks in empty theaters, small clubs, etc., the teenage group watched and learned. "Finally we met a young guy called Helinho who lived in a big house in the Cosme Velho quarter just beside the little train that climbs Corcovado Mountain to the famous Christ statue. Behind the house was a big covered veranda where the training sessions were resumed. People started showing up to watch. A *roda* became regular every Saturday evening." Soon, with less than two years of capoeira and no mestre, the young capoeiristas started to give classes, "teaching the little we knew to other kids."

Little by little the group grew: Itamar, Maranhão, Fausto "Borracha," Mosquito, Preguiça and later Baiano Anzol (both from Salvador) who had been Bimba's pupils, Bigode, Sanfona, Caio, Bermuda, and me, Nestor (who up to then had been a pupil of Mestre Leopoldina). Some of these stayed for five or even ten years and then stopped, since it must be said that very little money could be made with capoeira at that time. Other players continued until today.

It was during this "growing" period that the group started to present itself in clubs, theaters, weekend fairs, and universities. "This was very important because the group started to get a reputation," said Rafa. "And although most of these presentations were for free, it gave the young players a very good feeling: they were propagating capoeira and at the same time they were a bit like 'stars,' enjoying great success and popularity among their friends and especially among the girls."

Rafael notes the importance of "the contribution Preguiça and later on Baiano Anzol gave to the group. Preguiça came to Rio as part of Mestre Acordeon's successful show from Bahia in which capoeira was one of the highlights. The show went back to Salvador but Preguiça, around twenty years old at that time, stayed in Rio with Senzala, and the group absorbed even more of Bimba's style and teaching method."

Baiano Anzol arrived a couple of years later, not with a show but fleeing from a jealous husband who had already shot (and missed) him twice. "The influence of Capoeira Regional, the new training methods that the Senzala youngsters created and implanted, as well as the hard and energetic daily training started to show results. The group slowly started to be noticed among the other few that constituted Rio's capoeira scene in the 1960s."

During one of its first presentations, the group chose a name for itself upon the inquiries of the club's manager. "We also decided to wear pants similar to the ones in Rugendas' 1824 drawing of capoeira, with a red rope used as a belt around the waist," says Rafa. Thus the trademarks of the group—the name Senzala and the *corda-vermelha*—came on the scene with very little premeditation.

In the last years of the 1960s, Senzala structured itself in the veranda behind Helinho's house in Cosme Velho. To Bimba's *sequência* and *cintura desprezada* was added systematic repetition of kick training, using the outstretched hand of a partner as target. We also methodically trained two by two, repeating again and again the same blow and counter-blow, blow and swipe, etc. This mechanical repetition done for hours every day was something new. There were also a lot of push-ups and exercises for the stomach muscles, and the bodies and the technique of the young men started to change and improve rapidly.

Because we did not have a senior teacher, we began to create new forms of training.

We adapted routines seen in martial art academies, particularly karate, which was enjoying a big success in Rio with the arrival of the highly developed black belt, Tanaka, of the Shotokan style. All of this combined with the fact that we were young white guys from the upper middle class who had no contact with Afro-Brazilian culture (*candomblé, samba,* etc.) resulted in a quick development of the kicking technique and a very objective capoeira that was, in a certain way, little by little moving away from capoeira's original roots and turning itself into a sport-fighting technique.

Notwithstanding this lack of "roots," capoeira seems to have its own ways, and many of the young *"cordas-vermelhas"* started to spend time in Salvador taking classes and playing at Mestre Bimba's, Mestre Pastinha's, and at the traditional Sunday *roda* of Mestre Valdemar in the Liberdade quarter.

Meanwhile in Rio, the influence of Mestre Leopoldina, former teacher of Bermuda and myself (Nestor), was also being felt by the group. Slowly the style of playing started to change due to the influence of older players.

Rafael tells us that then something unexpected happened. "In 1967 at a big annual fair, a prize was created called the *'Berimbau de Ouro'* [Gold Berimbau] for the best capoeira group to present itself." The youngsters from Senzala together with their friend Helio Tabosa entered the contest just to gain experience. "It was a big surprise for us when we came out first among the eight or nine groups," says Rafael. One of the judges was Mestre Artur Emidio, the most respected capoeira player living in Rio at that time.

"In 1968 and '69," relates Rafael, "we repeated the feat, winning the Berimbau de Ouro definitively. The group then started to be known and talked about in São Paulo and Salvador."

I would like to add to Rafael's historical summary that mestres and more experienced players from Salvador would come to visit the Senzala trainings in Rio and were very impressed for several reasons.

First, there were three or four classes a day given by different *cordas-vermelhas*, each with fifteen to twenty students. In Salvador not even Bimba or Pastinha had that number of students.

Second, everybody was wearing the Senzala "uniform" (white *abada* trousers reaching just below the knees, the rope at the waist, no t-shirt, and barefoot), which gave the impression of something "very organized."

Third, the attitude of the students toward the teachers was a respectful one similar to the attitude of judo or karate students, or to the respect Bimba or Pastinha received from their pupils. In Bahia, many young guys who practiced capoeira for two or three years, not really giving their sweat and blood to the trainings, considered themselves already an expert—it is said as a joke that there are no "indians" in the Salvador capoeira "tribe" because everybody is a "chief"!

Fourth, there was a real togetherness among those ten or twelve *cordas-vermelhas* in the 1960s, while in Bahia the teachers, even when friends, always maintained a sly, wary attitude toward their "competitors"—due to capoeira's traditional *malícia*.

Fifth, and maybe most impressive: each pupil paid four times more than the ones in Salvador, not to say that each month it was a battle for Salvador teachers to collect the fee because many students gave excuses, paid late, etc.

To summarize: In Rio, as well as São Paulo, there was something really "professional" in the capoeira scene compared to Salvador. And when confronted with this new picture, Bahia's capoeira players and mestres reluctantly gave in to the idea that capoeira was not exclusively "Bahia." In São Paulo and Rio (and later in many other towns) something very impressive was happening.

This perception was enhanced when Bahia's capoeira teachers and mestres traveled or moved to Rio or São Paulo. Upon returning home for vacations, they seemed "different," with "big-city" points of view and mannerisms.

We must not forget that we are talking about the 1960s in Brazil. Although the hippie influence with the "tune in, turn on, drop out" attitude was being felt all over the world, Brazil was living a radical, right-wing, nationalistic military dictatorship (1964 to 1984) very much in tune with and sponsored by the USA. This dictatorship was in great part supported by the middle class (the bourgeoisie), as well as a large sector of the lower economic classes (those who were deadly afraid of communism).

Thus "order and progress," the slogan written on the Brazilian flag, was the "politically correct" motto of those times, as we have today's "ecology," "equal rights for men, women, and minorities," etc. So Rio's Senzala, with its young and fit players who didn't give a shit about politics, was paradoxically very much in tune with high- and middle-class values. The youngsters from Senzala also represented a return to "Brazilian Cultural Patrimony," which was in tune with the nationalistic right-wing policy of the military dictatorship. These factors surely contributed to Senzala's great success.

A few years later in the early '70s, according to Rafael's lecture, Senzala was firmly established in the capoeira world. When Helinho's house was demolished (today there is a public square on the site), the group moved on to a large ballroom at the Associação dos Servidores Civis club in the Botafogo quarter just off Copacabana Beach. Some years later, when they also had to vacate the Associação room, each *corda-vermelha* (now already called "mestre" though we were not yet thirty years old) started giving classes at his own place.

From the outside, Senzala looked like a solid and evolving group (it was the biggest in Brazil in the 1970s), with players at a very high technical level. But in fact the unity that existed when we were young had shattered. Many remained friends, but competition for students and status inside and outside the group was already having a negative effect.

By 1980 the "golden years" were already behind us, although from the outside and for newcomers Senzala retained its power and allure, especially because Bimba had died (1900–1974) and Pastinha (1889–1981) was blind and alone. The Senzala style of playing and the group's teaching method had influenced most capoeira teachers and academies in Brazil. For better or worse, Senzala's group infrastructure as well as its power relations also were copied. This included competition among teachers but a united front against the "outer world"; the obligatory "uniform" and hierarchy; the respectful teacher-pupil relationship similar to judo or karate; and the tendency of higher-ranked (high-*corda*) students to look down upon beginners. In fact, the influence of Senzala had started to become a problem by 1980. Everybody, everywhere, was playing in a similar way—the Senzala style. The only difference was that some played better than others.

Capoeira was becoming a mechanized, robotic, and repetitive form (due to the increasingly rigid teaching methodology), requiring a highly developed body and well-trained movement skills.

Rafael commented that very few *cordas-vermelhas* were graduated in the twenty years between 1964 and 1984 (year of the conference) in comparison to the thousands of pupils that went through the group: Paulinho, Lua "Rasta" (who came via Salvador as an experienced player), Muzenza, Claudio Moreno, Arara, Mula, and more recently Nagô, Capixaba, Jelon Vieira, and Toni Vargas. This high-quality standard, high-level technical playing, and love for capoeira have made Senzala one of the best-known and respected capoeira groups, he concluded.

Senzala's experience showed that it is more complicated to reach conclusions and to establish goals in a group when there isn't one "chief" to dictate the rules. Each *corda-vermelha* has different ways of thinking and being. Nevertheless, due to Senzala's success in the capoeira scene, we can say that a non-central and democratic system is possible and can deliver excellent results.

Finally, to update in 2002: Original members from the early 1960s still active in Senzala include: Gato and his brother "Gil Velho," Garrincha, Sorriso (in Montpelier, France), Peixinho, and Itamar. Preguiça began his own group and teaches in California. Lua "Rasta" went to Europe and now lives and teaches in Salvador. Mosquito died.

Among those who joined at the end of the 1960s, all left capoeira except Baiano Anzol and me (Nestor), both finally leaving Senzala in the 1990s after more than twenty years in the group.

Regarding the others who "grew up" in Senzala up to 1984: Paulinho Sabiá, Paulão, and Boneco left to start "Capoeira Brasil"; Camisa left in the 1990s and began Abada; Jelon Vieira now teaches in New York; Muzenza was shot dead; Capixaba and Nagô are with Abada; and Toni Vargas continues in Senzala.

A few other red-ropes have been graduated since 1984: Ramos, Luis Paulo (who left Senzala), Marron (who left Senzala and opened his own group), Feijão, Beto—all of them Peixinho's students (Rui, teaching in Copenhagen, should soon reach the red-rope level). Elias, who was introduced by Itamar, graduated from Senzala, and some of Garrincha's students soon (after more than twenty years in Senzala) should also become *corda-vermelhas:* Samara and Grilo (both in Amsterdam), Paulinho Boa-Vida (in Paris), and Bruzzi (in Montpelier, France).

After Rafael's speech came the questions and debates.

Somebody asked if a mere one or two years of capoeira was sufficient time to be able to give classes, as occurred in the early days of Senzala around 1964. Rafa answered that at that time they were simply a group of teenagers training capoeira, with no expectations of being or becoming a "teacher." They trained with each other, and if someone appeared and wanted to learn, they taught the little they knew.

Someone else asked how he could "affiliate himself with Senzala." Rafa answered that this sort of "affiliation" (which is normal procedure with the Capoeira Confederation) does not exist in Senzala. Whoever wants to belong to the group should become a pupil of one of the "red-ropes," who will give him a "rope" according to Senzala's standard and independent of any graduation the newcomer might have had in his previous group. With time he would move from one "rope" to the next. To get the red rope he would have to be approved by all the other "red-ropes" and not just by his own teacher.

Rafael also said that people had a tendency to place Senzala "against" the Capoeira Confederation, but this antagonism does not exist. In fact, he and many others from Senzala "had been the first to work on behalf of the creation of a Confederation many years ago." However, after Senzala's "red-ropes" experimented with many things during the twenty years between 1964 and 1984, including "capoeira championships," "competitive capoeira," and "sport capoeira," they came to the conclusion that they wanted to do "a sort of capoeira similar to the one passed from mestre to pupil through different generations. This is the capoeira practiced by Bimba and Pastinha and so many others who are no longer with us. Due to this, Senzala needed to do its work independently from the Federations and the CND [National Sport Council, a government organization]. They were ready to help the Federations and the Confederation in whatever way possible, but without losing their independence."

"These last twenty years [1964–1984]," Rafa concluded, "were not a 'sea of roses' as many players might think. Among other things it was always very difficult to find a training space."

Rafael added, "Assistance from the government or any other institution has been zero through all these years excepting INACEN's help on this meeting at the Circo Voador. And inside the group itself there are many different and conflicting ideas, discussions, and even fights, which is something that those from outside do not even suspect."

Notwithstanding all the troubles, Senzala survived as a group— a very special group with no "chief." Its older members are self-taught, learning from each other, learning by watching older and more experienced players, and adapting training routines from other contexts.

"The secret of Senzala's strength and endurance," Rafael said, "is that despite all the differences of personality and opinion, all the players had something in common: a great passion for the capoeira game."

ART AND SCIENCE IN CAPOEIRA

Ricardo Pena Machado, nicknamed "Macaco" (monkey), started capoeira in 1970. By 1974 he was part of a "technical study committee" on Minas Gerais' capoeira. Macaco graduated in physical education, and in 1979 and '80 earned a master's degree in the USA. He developed a teaching method called "Grupal" ("being part of the group") based on art-science integration applied to capoeira.

As for his "teaching method," I think it is similar to others found in Salvador, Rio, São Paulo, and elsewhere. Its main difference is that it graduates teachers of a lower level in less time (if compared with Senzala), and these new teachers automatically become partners (in the economic sense of the word) in the Ginga group. In 1984, there was a sense of "togetherness" and structure in this group, which was well-established in a beautiful house in the richest part of Belo Horizonte (Mina Gerais' capital). They were doing very well money-wise and capoeira-wise. Later, Macaco would go to Brasília and pursue other interests. The Ginga group changed but still exists in Belo Horizonte as a smaller group among many.

Macaco noted that "many times art and science are considered opposites." Then he called our attention to these questions: "What is capoeira? Art? Science? Folklore?"

He explained that art depends on science. To do a capoeira *roda* "one needs a certain knowledge, and it is this knowledge that we call 'science.' In the case of capoeira this science would be 'folklore,' 'folk' meaning people and 'lore' meaning knowledge."

Capoeira's scientific base would thus be "folklore," the people's knowledge, and Macaco explained that for something to be "folklore" it must have five qualities:

- It must be anonymous (it cannot have a known author but belongs to the people in general or to those who practice it);

- It must be accepted collectively (by the people);

- It relies on oral transmission (from father to son, or from teacher to pupil);

- It must be traditional;

- It must have a function (because everything done by the people has a reason, a goal, and a function).

Since capoeira fulfills these five requirements it is considered in the academic world to be folklore, "science or knowledge of the people."

After defining capoeira from this academic point of view, Macaco talked a bit about art and how Erich Fromm defined five qualities needed for someone to master an art: knowledge (practical and theoretic), determination, patience, concentration, and sensitivity.

"Contrary to what many think," Macaco continued, "everybody uses science in their everyday life, especially through a method known as 'trial and error.' The beginner who wants to master capoeira also uses this method intuitively: he tries several times to do the *aú* [cartwheel], for example, and his mind separates what was 'correct' from the 'mistakes,' and slowly the *aú* improves."

Then Macaco talked about the main "sciences of movement" that can be applied to capoeira: physiology of force, motor skill, and biomechanics. A practical example of the use of physiology is the different stretching and warm-up methods. Other practical applications relate, for example, to the care of the knees. Doing stretching exercises with your legs wide open and both feet "planted" on the ground could damage the knee. These exercises should be done with the heels on the ground and the feet pointing upward.

Macaco also talked about the body's "gravity center," explaining that "these concepts are important if we scientifically study capoeira's movements in order to find out how each one can be done with the most 'technique' (that is, less effort and more efficiency)."

Macaco concluded, "Science can contribute increasingly to those who practice capoeira, but it is important to put things in their proper places: science can help, support, and contribute to the capoeira art but it should never dominate or restrain such an art."

Then came the questions.

Paulão from Fortaleza (now teaching in Holland and head of "Capoeira Brasil" together with Mestres Boneco and Paulinho Sabiá) asked what would be the most important motor skills for capoeira. Macaco's answer was neuro-muscular coordination and agility (which also means "capacity to conquer fear"). Strength, for example, isn't so important because it is inversely proportional to "technique" (greatest efficiency with the least effort).

Camisa said that one of the capoeirista's greatest problems is the knees. What could be done about that? Macaco explained that it is possible to do therapy on the muscles but not on the knee ligaments. He recommends isometric exercises as recuperation and to strengthen the knee: holding up weights for 5 to 15 seconds with the leg horizontally stretched out and then bending the knee only 15°—that is, the foot goes down about the span of one hand. We should not let the foot drop totally down when bending the knee.

Someone who was studying physiotherapy said, "It's dangerous to teach people how to treat or medicate themselves without seeking the professional advice of a specialist." Macaco answered, "You are right as far as theory is concerned. But the truth is that most capoeiristas don't have the money to obtain a doctor [public health and public hospitals in Brazil do not function at all], and I am simply talking, as one capoeirista to another, about basic practices that could contribute to a science that belongs to the people and to those who practice it."

Edna, graduated *mestra* from Mestre Tabosa's academy in Brasília (she is now teaching in New York), said that she worried about body-building becoming a fashion. "Many people have spine and vertebrae problems and are working with heavy weights," she noted. She asked if body-building was good for capoeira players, and if there was a limit.

Macaco answered, "Today we have a wholesome mentality of taking care of the body, but to be respected because of your body might not be such a wholesome idea. Muscle-building can complement the capoeirista's training, but it must never be his main focus."

He added that it was not as useful as many thought. "As an example," he said, "we have the mulatto who traditionally was lighter and more malicious than the negro, and made better capoeira players."

This statement is likely a reference to writer Luis Edmundo's (1880–1961) book *O Rio de Janeiro do meu tempo* (Rio: Conquista, 1957). Edmundo gave a romantic picture of the nineteenth-century capoeira player:

> Without the negro's athletic build nor the Portuguese's healthy and stocky figure, the capoeirista is someone feared by all and Justice itself respects him ... all his strength is due to this amazing elastic dexterity that causes the slow European to hesitate and the astonished negro to lose his pace.

Scholars and writers, as well as other sectors of society, have always tried to create an "image" and an "identity" for the Brazilian man/woman. A very "politically correct" attitude in Edmundo's era was the idea of "mixed races": the "typical" Brazilian would be the result of mixed races.

This idea has survived several generations, and even today we find those who say that "Brazil is the cauldron from where will come a new race of mixed blood." Nevertheless there are scholars such as Muniz Sodré who criticize this posture, saying that while we continue to wait for this "new race" of mixed blood, the idea that every Brazilian is of mixed blood makes it logical to conclude that there is no racism in Brazil, thereby presenting a "clean and correct" image of Brazilian society.

Today (2002) we know that the romantic and attractive idea of "mixed blood" in Brazil, which is true to a very great extent, paradoxically can be used to screen the reality of a country with a big racist problem. And, as a consequence, we might say that the stereotyped idea of the mulatto being a better player than the (athletic, well-built) negro or the (slow and healthy) white because the mulatto is "more flexible and creative" (which is not true, as far as my experience has shown me) can also be used to eclipse capoeira's African roots, and to divide ("divide in order to conquer") mulattos from blacks and whites. (This was not the case with Macaco.)

Camisa commented that today many capoeiristas want to compensate for their lack of technique with brute force, and that "they look like an island: a bunch of muscles encircled by ignorance on all sides."

Perna, from Rio, commented that abdominal exercises were done for many years with the legs stretched out, and this caused problems in the spinal column. These exercises should always be done with flexed knees, with the feet on the ground or in the air.

Macaco brought up one last issue. He said that some doctors think "warming up" before doing any sport or physical labor has a function that is more psychological than "material." As far as the human body itself is concerned, "if you played capoeira 'cold' [without a warm-up] but motivated mentally and emotionally, this can be as good as doing a long warm-up before the game."

WOMEN IN CAPOEIRA

This presentation was the result of several meetings among the women players from the Senzala group. They chose as speakers Marcia and Luísa (Camisa's students), Morena (Peixinho's student), and Edna (mestra from Tabosa's academy in Brasília and a karate black belt).

Edna spoke about women's long struggle throughout many generations in order to have equal rights in relation to men. "More than 3,000 years ago, in Old Greece, already women's role was similar to the slave's. They should have children and raise them, take care of the weaving and the food, but they had no access to activities linked to thought and knowledge."

Edna continued by telling us, "In 625 B.C. the poet Sappho opened her school for women, and this was one of the first moves toward a dynamic position in society. There have been other exceptional cases such as in old Germany, where there were two tribal societies in which women's status was similar to men's and they took part in the tribe's councils, in judging lawsuits, and in war. In London in the fourteenth century we find fifteen women graduated by the university and practicing medicine. In America's eighteenth century there was a strong movement where many women had a leading role."

Edna said that in 1974 when she was twelve she had never heard of capoeira when the game began to be taught in her school. Immediately she perceived that it was "forbidden to women," so she obtained money from home on the pretense of buying a book, in order to avoid telling her parents. She enrolled herself in the class without their knowledge. After one month she started to worry about being "the only girl among boys." She told her mother about the capoeira classes, and fortunately her mother supported her. But there was a "strong reaction from the rest of the family and neighbors, who insisted that capoeira was for men and even for bandits."

Edna and her mother struggled with these prejudices and society's mediocre values. She trained a long time without meeting another female capoeirista, and if, on one hand, she was accepted by her fellow capoeiristas, on the other she endured a lot of jokes at the Saturday night teenage parties she went to.

Edna commented on the "excessive competition between players, men and women alike, most of them seeking some sort of self-affirmation using brute force and violence in order 'not to lose.' This contradicts the basic point of any martial art, which is to preserve the physical integrity of one's opponent." Edna concluded, "It's no good to train violent blows in order to arrive at a *roda* to show one is 'the strongest'."

Edna thanked her mestre, Helio Tabosa, "for the contribution he gave to my psychological, physical, and emotional development."

After Edna's comments came Luísa, journalist and capoeira player, who spoke about the difficulty in tracing women's performance in capoeira, as there is so little available material. "Nonetheless, tradition tells us about women warriors in the Quilombo dos Palmares [a runaway slaves' colony in the jungle] in the eighteenth century," Luísa noted. Other women "who left their name and legend in Bahia's capoeira history" include Rosa Palmeirão, Maria "Cabaço," and Maria Doze Homens [Twelve Men]—"all women who lived in the lawless underground world similar to other capoeiristas as well as all black culture and black people of those times."

"Maria Cabaço always got involved in fights and lived by herself without a mate, and that is the reason for her nickname [*cabaço* is a rude term for 'virgin']. It is said that she had a lot of problems with her physical appearance. Rosa Palmeirão was a well-known street fighter."

Luísa recalled that Bimba trained his daughters as capoeiristas, so women in capoeira is at least as old as the first capoeira academies (in the 1930s). She noted two mestras active in 1984: Edna in Brasília and Sandrinha in the Favela do Pavãozinho (a slum in the hills of Copacabana, Rio), "who have been doing their work for some time already."

Luísa also criticized the "lack of union" among women capoeira players. She said, "There is a lack of maturity and an excess of competitiveness. A woman capoeirista should be the first to support other women in the capoeira world, but many times that doesn't happen." Then she showed a 1930s photo provided by Mestre Jair Moura (a former pupil of Bimba and author of several excellent books on capoeira) in which several women led by Mestre Bimba are shown training capoeira in a back yard.

Morena spoke next, giving the example of two female capoeiristas who gave an interview to a newspaper in which they said that their goal was to become mestres, a goal shared by most players, men and women alike. But they worried that "most women would prefer a male mestre." These young women were "absolutely sure" that men would not choose a female mestra. Morena echoed the sentiment that most women in the capoeira world felt insignificant and unsupported.

Morena concluded by saying, "The presentation we are going to perform tonight is very important to show that women have conquered a space in capoeira as a result of their dedication and training." She noted that in rehearsals there had been a lot of dispute and discussion, but the women managed to bypass those problems "to show they deserve the space conquered in capoeira and in Senzala."

Other women players agreed that aggression and excessive competition exist between women in capoeira, but they consider this the legacy of "a certain type of education and the position women were relegated in society and only very recently began to change." The women players believe that "through meetings, discussions, and women's capoeira *rodas*" they are educating themselves "to improve this state of things."

During the question and debate session that followed, many women players from Rio and other states expressed their solidarity and support. At that very moment during the discussion, members of the *"velha guarda"* (senior mestres, the "old guard") arrived at the conference from Salvador and the airport.

Morena posed the question to them that was on everybody's mind: what did the *velha guarda* think of the participation of women in the capoeira movement?

João Pequeno, one of the most respected mestres of Capoeira Angola and one of the best-known players of Pastinha's academy (Mestre Pastinha died three years earlier, in 1981), answered, "Women have a human body as do men, and women feel the same thing. Perhaps they need capoeira more than men because women have less physical strength." He received a standing ovation when he concluded: "In capoeira, I consider all persons as equals."

That evening, the presentation of the female Senzala pupils of Toni, Sorriso, Garrincha, Camisa, and Peixinho, together with Edna from Brasília, was spectacular. The audience at Circo Voador became very excited and moved by the *maculelê* with *"grimas"* (wooden sticks) and machetes, and the *atabaque* playing and singing.

Afterwards the twenty capoeiristas, ranging from 15 to 25 years old, did a choreography with capoeira movements, performed solos, played berimbau and sang, and played Angola style as well as the objective and fast game at the *"são bento grande"* rhythm. It was a great show.

Some old, stereotyped ideas crumbled. The first was that capoeira is only for men. Another was the fear that capoeira practice might "masculinize" women. All who saw that dream-team doing their performance were mesmerized.

It was clear that prejudice against women in capoeira exists and is very strong in society as well as in certain academies. On the other hand, in other academies (some of the best known for their high level) there is no problem accepting women among the students and players.

THE CAPOEIRA FEDERATION

João Mulatinho was a young man in 1984 but was already President of Pernambuco's Boxing and Fighting Federation (a governmental organ). He served as Chief of the Capoeira Department of this same Federation in 1979.

Mulatinho was a pupil of the deceased Mosquito and Gil Velho, both from Senzala's original group in Rio in the early 1960s. He went to Recife, the largest city in Brazil's Northeast and capital of Pernambuco state, in his early twenties and was one of the first to definitively establish capoeira in the area. Two of his pupils, Corisco and Berilo, are presently (2002) mestres of two of the most important groups of that region.

(Another player who had a great influence on Recife's capoeira during the same period, especially the "street capoeira" of the young and tough kids, was Mestre Teté, who now lives and teaches in Switzerland, and his former student, Mestre Barrao, who now teaches in Vancouver, Canada.)

Mulatinho's topic was the Capoeira Federation, though he said it was not easy to talk about because most of the players at the meeting were not affiliated with the Federation. Nonetheless, he offered to present "a general idea of Brazil's sport system and the role assumed by the Federations."

At the very top of the hierarchy is the President of Brazil followed by the Ministry of Education and Culture. Then the chain of authority passes to the National Sports Council, the Confederations (private nationwide entities), the Federations (private statewide entities), and finally the Associations (academies affiliated with their state Federation).

"The Federation's role is to inspect, supervise, and support the Associations [academies]."

Some states already had Capoeira Federations, and those that didn't had a Capoeira Department inside the Boxing and Fighting Federation. At the time (1984) all capoeira Federations and Departments were supervised by the national Boxing and Fighting Confederation, explained Mulatinho. The (national) Capoeira Confederation had not yet been created in 1984, but a few years later this entity evolved. Today there is a national Capoeira Confederation along with capoeira federations in each state. While many groups have affiliated themselves and use this graduation system, the Confederation as a whole has not done any particularly notable work for capoeira over the past 15 years, despite the increase in membership. Most presidents of state federations and especially the Brazilian Capoeira Confederation have not been globally known players and often are not even leaders of a major group. They frequently do not play the berimbau or possess expressive singing skills. As predicted, many have bureaucratic minds and attempt to "organize" or exert power over capoeira (without much success!). Countless hours are wasted in petty debate or confrontation, over the Internet or in the pages of journals. That's the Capoeira Federations.

Mulatinho asserted, "Since 1982 capoeira has been registered by the CND [National Sports Council] and has had to fit into the existing hierarchy for a very simple reason: it is the law." In the debates that followed it became clear that capoeira must fit into this hierarchy only for those who want to teach it as a sport with championships legally recognized by the government.

Mulatinho reminded us that capoeira is officially registered as "Brazil's national sport," explaining what is necessary for something to be considered a sport: it must be a physical activity with a competition following certain rules. Thus for capoeira to be "sport" it must have championships. Those not participating in the championships would have their capoeira classified as "recreational activity" and would not be part of the jurisdiction of the National Sports Council.

In order to install a state Federation (there can be only one for each state) there must exist three legally functioning Associations (academies), explained Mulatinho. To legalize an academy as an Association, the mestre has to deliver a statute (found in the Boxing Federations of each state), register the statute properly, have it published by the National Press, and then go to the local CRD (Regional Sports Council) and ask for the Association paper. "It's a simple process but it takes time and money."

Once a state's Federation is established, only the affiliated Associations can take part in the championships organized by this Federation.

"This is a problem for the poorer states [a great part of the Northeast of Brazil is extremely poor] because many teachers don't have the money to carry out the bureaucratic tasks necessary to transform an academy into an Association," noted Mulatinho. "A good solution is to look for a soccer team belonging to the Soccer Confederation and create a Capoeira Department in the soccer team." With this bypass, one's academy could be affiliated with the Federation without spending time or money.

Then Mulatinho gave a general panorama in relation to academies that have become Associations. "In Bahia the situation was out of control, in Rio few academies had affiliated themselves, and in São Paulo they also had problems." But he thought that the Federations and the future Confederation that would lead capoeira out of the Boxing Confederation was "the best way for capoeira, although at the present moment (1984) the situation is a bit confused."

[By 2002, the Confederation had managed to mainly organize capoeira championships, which have gradually lost their appeal to most capoeiristas. To its credit, the Confederation has sponsored and organized the JEBS, a championship for teens that has motivated many young players. Yet even this event has drawn criticism for unfair choices, etc.]

Creation of a national Capoeira Confederation required three state Federations with the role of "inspecting, orientating, supervising, and supporting the Associations."

"This is the way," Mulatinho asserted, "notwithstanding all the present problems, which include the fact that the technical rules are old and do not work, the hierarchic system is outdated, the championship rules malfunction, and the system that upgrades teachers into mestres is really bad."

Mulatinho proposed that each teacher turn his academy into an Association or open a Capoeira Department in a soccer club upon returning home from the conference. Together with two other Associations they could start a state Federation (if it didn't already exist). "Despite the present chaotic situation, we can start working together. With time and by voting in the general meetings, everything could be changed."

In his opinion, "What can't continue is what we see at the moment: it's important that capoeira players start to occupy more space inside the Boxing and Fighting Confederation [which makes all the rules] until we manage to start the Capoeira Confederation."

He said he believed that it was possible to create "championship rules that do not go against capoeira's *fundamentos* [foundations, roots]" and reaffirmed, "Basically, capoeira is a fight." Mulatinho had contacted several soccer teams in Recife in order to create Capoeira Departments, and they organized some championships with "excellent results." In Recife a great many of the best players and teachers were affiliated with the Federation, "making it strong," but that had not happened in Rio and São Paulo. Mulatinho said it was important that "the best players and the best brains" were not only affiliated but were the leaders of each Federation.

He said that in the championships, "We had physical contact as in any form of fighting, but the physical integrity of the players was protected." By contrast, in the *rodas* "we only have some highly technical *floreio* and if you make contact, a *benção* in the chest for example, the game turns into a street fight with no rules. As far as I'm concerned," Mulatinho added, "notwithstanding the *floreio*, capoeira is a form of fighting."

He concluded by saying that if the capoeiristas didn't do anything when they returned home, "we will continue to depend on some organism alien to us." He noted that in this particular 1984 meeting we were lucky to be supported by the Circo Voador and INACEN (the National Scenic Arts Institute) but that was not always possible. The Federations "have to be independently functioning with their own funds, and this will only be possible when there are many players and academies affiliated." (Funds for the Federations come from the dues charged to affiliated Associations.)

"Sport is important, competition is important, and establishing rules is important," said Mulatinho, "and the championships can do all of this."

As was the conference's format, questions and debates followed the presentation.

Mestre Itapoan said, "Bahia withdrew from the Capoeira Federation due to the lack of competence in the Board of Directors. Several meetings were held with the Boxing and Fighting Confederation, and decisions were made to change the old, non-applicable rules of the capoeira championships. The Boxing and Fighting Confederation [which oversees Bahia's Capoeira Federation] gave the excuse that they lost the transcripts of the meetings, and the championship was held with the old, obsolete rules instituted by the Boxing and Fighting Confederation."

Mulatinho answered that the Boxing and Fighting Confederation was "obliged to follow the decisions of the general meetings, and the story of the lost transcripts is inconceivable. For cases like this we have the Sport Justice Council." He said that the future solution was "not to vote in incompetent directors."

Mestre Gato, one of Senzala's founders, said, "Mulatinho asserted that capoeira has been qualified as sport [by the CND, the National Sports Council] but I disagree." As far as he was concerned, capoeira is "art, a way of living life, and any institution that would oversee capoeira should be something entirely new, created specifically for capoeira." He gave the movies as an example. When motion pictures first appeared "they wanted to classify them as 'photography' or 'theatre,' things that already existed." But later, specific institutions such as Embrafilmes and the INC (National Cinema Institute) were created. Gato then noted, "A Capoeira Confederation is not the solution because it belongs to the CND arena, and to practice capoeira as a sport having championships as its final goal makes the capoeirista limited, crude, and stupid." He added that in capoeira we have rules, but they are "subtle and subjective." Gato finished by saying, "Whoever plays capoeira thinking of 'winning' kills capoeira."

Mulatinho answered that the idea was interesting but impossible to realize once capoeira had officially been defined as "sport." Thus it was inside the Federations "that we have to fight for our objectives."

Gato again disagreed. He could not create a "capoeira sport institution" outside the Federations and the CND's area of influence, but if it were necessary he could register his academy as "something with 'artistic and cultural purposes' or in the 'amusement' arena" and practice his capoeira the way he wanted, as he had received it "from the old mestres of past times."

Mestre Camisa (the main organizer of the meeting) spoke up. "The Federations only exist if there are capoeira players affiliated with them. If the players don't affiliate, there is no Federation." He added that if the "men" [big brass, bureaucrats] instituted a law saying that "whether you want it or not, capoeira is a sport, then we are going to leave the 'men' all alone with their law." Thus an institution from the sports arena "would never be able to organize capoeira properly." Camisa thought Gato was right but "if it is impossible to create something new specifically for capoeira, then we will again go underground [as in the 1890–1930 period]." He said that capoeira had already been outlawed in the past and had survived for more than four centuries, and "it was not sport that was going to kill it."

Mestre João Pequeno, a main figure in Salvador's Angola *velha guarda,* said that he agreed that capoeira can be a sport, but only (and this is his main worry) "if nothing is taken away from her and this [sport designation] serves as a means of making it bigger."

Mestre Canjiquinha, also from Salvador's *velha guarda,* said, "If we take the berimbau away from capoeira, it is sport, but with the berimbau, capoeira is capoeira."

Mestre Paulo dos Anjos, from a slightly younger generation than João Pequeno and Canjiquinha, explained that he knew a bit about the Boxing and Fighting Confederation because he had been a professional boxer. Paulo made an ironic remark about the organization's board of directors: "It's like picking a butcher to be president of the Shoemakers Syndicate because the shoes' soles are made of cow leather."

I, Nestor Capoeira, spoke up and said, "I see two different approaches. But the one proposed by Mulatinho with the Capoeira Confederation and the championships should not hinder the capoeiristas who consider capoeira to be something different from sport. These other players should be able to assemble themselves under an 'artistic and cultural' banner if they wish." I concluded, "These two approaches don't have to be antagonistic; they can parallel one another, helping and completing the other's work." I explained how these "artistic and cultural entities" could get money from governmental cultural institutions as well as from private companies and industries, as in Europe and the USA. This was already happening in Brazil in the artistic arena, as was the case of the Circo Voador itself being sponsored by an oil company. In the sports arena, football and volleyball are often sponsored by private industries.

Mulatinho was interested but said such sponsorship was only likely to happen in the South of Brazil, "which is richer." He believed it would be impossible in the Northeast. He thought that there should be "general rules for everyone and only one central institution to delegate them to all of Brazil."

I disagreed, saying that in my opinion, "the least centralized power, with the greatest liberty of action for each mestre, would be better."

Mestre Itapoan said that it is possible to create "artistic-cultural entities" such as those described. "In fact, there is already one related to the culture/sport area, the ABPC [Brazilian Capoeira Teachers Association], founded and registered in 1981. This Association's point of view is very broad, and it would never persecute, for example, the *'rodas de ruas'* [street *rodas*], which are a very rich part of popular culture. The *roda de rua* is similar to the *pelada* [informal soccer games played in the streets, squares, beaches, etc.], and that's where you truly 'make' capoeira players."

Mestre Macaco, from Belo Horizonte, said that he had served as vice-president of a sport Federation and "whoever thinks that through the Federations or a Confederation capoeira will receive any financial help or support is completely misinformed. Capoeira was officially registered as 'sport' in 1972 and what has been done [by the government or other institutions] to support it? Nothing!"

Mestre Martins, from Rio, said that in his opinion, "The Rio de Janeiro Capoeira Federation is the biggest thing that has happened to Rio's capoeira in many, many years. This Federation is only four months old [in 1984] and is like a child learning to walk." Martins then expressed disappointment because Mulatinho "created a list of names for the kicks valid for the state of Pernambuco notwithstanding an official list already existing for all of Brazil." Martins also was disappointed because "This meeting was organized with the help of INACEN and the Circo Voador, leaving Rio's Capoeira Federation out." However, he thanked his friend Camisa for inviting him and his group to do an exhibition at the meeting.

Rafael, from Rio's Senzala, mentioned once again Senzala's position in regard to the Federations: "The Federations are taking care of the sport part of capoeira, and Senzala and many other players are taking care of other parts. There shouldn't be antagonism, but activities should augment one another." Camisa confirmed Rafa's sentiments and insisted on the creation of a specific institute for capoeira, independent from the sports realm.

Perfeito Fortuna, one of Circo Voador's directors, wrapped it up: "This circus is something very 'bizarre' because it doesn't fit in any of the existing 'official' categories. Nonetheless, the Circo Voador exists, it is real, and has been successful for several years. Capoeira in Brazil is much older than the laws that want to rule it. Capoeira is much more than dance, fighting, or sport, and something entirely new must be created to support it. The people are the ones who understand capoeira, not these institutions that erect enormous structures and monuments full of air-conditioned rooms but don't have the money to support an old capoeira mestre who is living in misery. They build monuments but they don't support men."

CAPOEIRA IN THE UNITED STATES

Ubirajara de Almeida, a.k.a. Mestre Acordeon, was graduated by Mestre Bimba in the 1960s. After teaching and helping spread capoeira in Brazil for more than fifteen years, he went to the United States and began teaching in California in the late '70s.

Bira de Almeida (Mestre Acordeon) explained that his speech would focus on two aspects: capoeira's history in the US and how capoeira is seen in the US.

For Brazilians, his speech was interesting for two other reasons: many capoeiristas think of leaving Brazil and are curious about what they will find when they try to establish themselves in a foreign country. Furthermore, in capoeira's big picture, it was likely that we would see a great movement of capoeiristas from Brazil to Europe and America over the coming years, the same way there was a big movement from Salvador to Rio and São Paulo in the

1960s. It is not impossible that in the future capoeira's center will no longer be only Brazil but America and Europe as well—the same way capoeira's center was Salvador and by 1984 it was Salvador/Rio/São Paulo.

Mestre Acordeon said, "In 1974 Jelon Vieira, a former pupil of Mestre Ezequiel (also graduated by Mestre Bimba) arrived in America with a small group of capoeiristas to do shows. Jelon established himself in New York and is still there today [in 1984, when he was part of Senzala]. Some years later I arrived and established myself in California."

Mestre Acordeon felt the need to "preserve capoeira abroad the same way it originally was in Brazil." Having this in mind, he founded the World Capoeira Association (WCA), which was highly criticized in Salvador because of its name. "My colleagues didn't understand that this 'World' is only a name that functions well commercially, so there was a general commentary that 'capoeira is being robbed from Brazil'."

Mestre Acordeon explained that capoeira has no support in America and little recognition. In 1984 there were only about three hundred students in California, sixty in New York, and some one hundred scattered with other mestres [besides himself and Jelon]. "Preguiça [from Senzala in 1984] is one of these mestres who has recently arrived in the US."

Mestre Acordeon said that when he was younger he was very radical, but now he thinks "nobody owns capoeira, it belongs to everybody. Capoeira isn't only for athletes but also for old people, etc. The most important thing is the degree of satisfaction one has when playing and not his technical performance."

Mestre Acordeon says three things are important when you teach in a foreign country and want to be faithful to tradition: "Know the history and the roots, know the 'philosophy' of capoeira, and practice with discipline."

Regarding capoeira's history, Mestre Acordeon wrote a book published in the US (*Capoeira, A Brazilian Art Form*, North Atlantic Books) in which his pupils can find "the relatively small researched, documented, and known part of capoeira's history, as well as the theories of different people and groups."

As far as the roots are concerned, "it is important that American players get to know figures of capoeira's past such as Mestre Bimba and others." He said that on his previous trip to Brazil with a group of American students, he felt they had more respect for the *velha guarda* than the majority of Brazilian capoeiristas. Mestre Acordeon concluded, "'Mestre' does not mean the one who goes into the *roda* to compete and to win, but someone who knows capoeira deeply."

As far as capoeira's philosophy is concerned, he tried to "give practical examples as they arose in the classes, in the game, and in life itself."

Regarding the "practice with discipline," Mestre Acordeon has his own method. "There are different ways of becoming a good player and no method is 'the best.' Nevertheless, there are both good and bad teachers." Mestre Acordeon says capoeira should be a reflection of each person, and he is opposed to "mestres who want the pupils as a copy of themselves. Obviously we find common ingredients in the capoeira way of moving, but each player should express his/her personality and biotype tendencies."

During the ensuing questions and debates, Mestre Acordeon talked about things that break capoeira's tradition and ritual: a pupil buying the game when there is a mestre crouched at the foot of the berimbau waiting to play; or a pupil that buys the game of a mestre who is playing; or a pupil asking a mestre who is playing the berimbau to pass him the instrument. Mestre Itapoan (from Bahia and also a former pupil of Bimba) reinforced Mestre Acordeon's statement, telling the group that Mestre Valdemar da Liberdade, from the "old guard" of Capoeira Angola, told him, "This lack of respect, among other things, annoys me to a point that I don't fancy going to the *rodas* anymore."

Then Mestre Valdemar, who was also at the meeting, said he didn't agree with the World Capoeira Association created by Mestre

Acordeon in the US: "It's absurd that an international capoeira organization is based in the USA and not in Brazil."

Mestre Acordeon again explained that the "World" in the institution's name was just a word. "WCA is only a private and non-official organization created to help competent capoeiristas in the USA."

Mestre Gato asked if a Brazilian capoeirista who affiliated himself with the WCA could continue to use his original graduation system. Mestre Acordeon answered, "The WCA, like Senzala, has its own graduation system."

Mestre João Pequeno, one of the most important figures of Salvador's Angola *velha guarda,* said, "I too worry about the creation of an international association outside Brazil." He asked if someone who wanted to create another international association would have to affiliate himself with the WCA.

"The WCA is not an official entity but a private one," said Mestre Acordeon. "Anyone can create a new capoeira world association without any attachment to the WCA."

Somebody asked what type of American was attracted by capoeira.

"Different kinds of people," answered Mestre Acordeon, "those who are interested in martial arts, Afro-Americans searching for their roots, dancers (especially women interested in Latin dance), those who want to learn something coming from Brazil, and those who saw capoeira, liked it, and stayed." Mestre Acordeon explained that he was established in California, a state "with an open mentality. If I were in a state with a closed and conservative mentality, my work would be much more difficult."

He talked about his work at Stanford University. "After three years teaching I managed to get capoeira included in the university's curriculum, but the students—mostly from the middle and upper class—prefer other sports. They are not capoeira's clientele." He said that to become rich with capoeira in America (a dream of many Brazilian players) is an illusion. "Only a small part of the American population has any interest for another country's culture, and it is this minority that forms capoeira's clientele. And capoeira has to fight for this market with other 'exotic' arts coming from all over the world, especially in California and New York, where this American minority with interest in other cultures is mostly located. What helps capoeira to survive are the shows and presentations sponsored by the American government, which are not easy to arrange."

Mestre Lua "Rasta," a street capoeirista from Salvador and former pupil of Mestre Caiçaras who later earned Senzala's coveted red rope, had recently (in 1984) dedicated himself to building percussion instruments and doing a sort of "street theater" with his small group; performances embody several parts of Brazil's popular culture. He offered his opinion, saying, "Something like 'capoeira in the USA' is a sophisticated issue without a basic, wide-ranging interest among this group. Things like racism in capoeira and in Senzala, discrimination, and middle-class prejudice that deeply affect many mestres should be the issues discussed here."

Mestre Camisa, the meeting's main organizer, explained that the topic was chosen for one of the talks because "many capoeiristas are going to the USA, and in the future this could be resented by the capoeira practiced in Brazil. I think it's interesting that we know even now what goes on abroad so we can prepare ourselves for the future."

Mestre Gato said, "The issues pointed out by Lua are very important, and they will be on the next day's conference agenda."

Mestre Miguel, from Bahia, criticized the organization of the event, saying that he had come to the meeting "by myself and at my own expense, because the Rio Grande do Sul state is not represented here." But what he really wanted to talk about was "how many of the people in charge of our Federations are military or people who come from the Physical Education area—people who have nothing to do with capoeira and know nothing about Afro-Brazilian culture. In fact, these organizations are repressive entities interested in manipulating power. Does Mestre Acordeon's American WCA have the same problem and end result?"

Before Mestre Mestre Acordeon could answer, Mestre Atenilo, the only representative of Bimba's Regional among Salvador's *velha guarda,* brusquely interrupted and asked, "What capoeira secrets does the United States know?" He went on: "You know me, Mestre Acordeon. I came under Bimba's influence when I was twelve years old. All of you [who graduated from Bimba's academy] know me, and to tell you the truth, I haven't seen one single person who knows capoeira's secret! What is capoeira's secret, the one you must know to become a mestre? Tell me: in what article of law is it included?" Atenilo concluded: "I don't accept a World Capoeira Association in the United States. It belongs to Brazil, it is born in Brazil, and they will never know its secret!"

Mestre Acordeon broke the tension, saying to Atenilo that he had given him (Mestre Acordeon) "a *rasteira.*" Mestre Acordeon concluded, "If the name 'World' is creating so many problems, when I get back to the US, I will check the legal procedures to change my organization's name." Mestre Acordeon ended the night saying he was going to continue to "modestly divulge capoeira abroad with what I know and with what I learned from my mestre. And I will be there to help anyone who is competent."

In the following years Mestre Acordeon changed the name of his organization to "United Capoeira Association."

Here I should comment. Somewhere in this book I've already said that American capoeira is especially fortunate. There are good teachers in Europe now (2002), but they are all young, the oldest in their early forties. There is nothing like in the US, with Mestre João Grande, one of Pastinha's most renowned pupils, teaching on the East Coast and Mestre Bira "Acordeon," one of the most renowned of Bimba's pupils, teaching on the West Coast.

I speak not only of the quality of the game of these two men, or their deep knowledge and half a century of experience. It is the rare quality of generosity and friendship that they have provided and perfected throughout the years that ultimately makes them exceptional.

Mestre Atenilo is now dead, so I think it might be instructive to tell a little tale about the background of the surprising events that concluded Mestre Acordeon's talk on "Capoeira in the USA." Mestre Acordeon has kept silent about them, but I think this might be the proper time to bring them to light.

What did Atenilo mean by saying, "I haven't seen one single person who knows capoeira's secret!" What is capoeira's secret? Mestre Acordeon knew what Atenilo was talking about, but from respect, recognition, and friendship toward the older player, Mestre Acordeon remained silent and even said that, regarding the discussion around his World Capoeira Association, Atenilo "had given me [Mestre Acordeon] a *rasteira*." The "secret" Atenilo referred to was that capoeira had been forbidden by law in the Brazilian Republic's first Legal Code (1892), and this had been maintained until Dictator Vargas took power in the 1930s.

In fact, many capoeiristas around the 1950s didn't know about this dark period in capoeira's past—forbidden by law and persecuted by the police. And among the few that knew, they largely kept it a secret. This went on more or less until the 1960s, when books such as Waldeloir Rego's *Capoeira Angola* were first published. But even then this "secret" did not become a well-known and discussed fact because not even 5% of the existing players read books. Furthermore, many who did read thought that such information should not be propagated among the middle class/bourgeoisie, members of which had a great prejudice (much more in the 1960s than now) against capoeira and Afro-Brazilian culture in general.

Mestre Acordeon knew this, and so did many of the young mestres and teachers at the 1984 meeting. But Atenilo would have lost face if Mestre Acordeon said Atenilo's "secret" was now known by everyone with a little information on capoeira history. Mestre Acordeon kept quiet. And never again mentioned the subject in public, not even after Atenilo's death some years later.

It's easy to learn capoeira but it's difficult to play it well and really get to know it. It is even more difficult to be a true mestre such as Mestre Acordeon and Mestre João Grande, who presently live and teach in America, or like Mestre Leopoldina and Mestre João Pequeno, who live in Brazil.

CAPOEIRA IN BAHIA

Before Mestre Itapoan delivered his speech, Mestre Onça-tigre, an older player (well over 60 in 1984) from Bimba's lineage who introduced capoeira to Brasília, read a text that reviewed the arrival of the first Africans up to our days. (The night that Mestre Helio Tabosa, who went from Rio to Brasília and became one of the strongest capoeira references in the capital, gave an exhibition with his group, Onça-tigre in dark suit and tie stole the show by defending himself with an umbrella while Tabosa "attacked" him with a knife. Onça-tigre showed that some capoeiristas, similar to good wine, get better when they grow old.)

Mestre Itapoan, of a younger generation than Mestre Acordeon and also a former pupil of Bimba, started his speech by asking permission "from those who raised me in capoeira, and from the mestres of the past and the present, to talk about the history of capoeira in Bahia, which is deeply linked with the story of black people in Brazil."

He showed many slides from the historical artists Rugendas and Debret, drawn around the 1830s. He said, "Everyone should read these books because they are some of the few good sources about lifestyles as well as the fauna and the flora at the beginning of the nineteenth century, and the book can be found in many municipal libraries."

The drawings portray the ships of the slave trade, where all sort of diseases including *banto,* "the sickness of sorrow," took many victims. They portray the slave markets in Brazil where the Africans were sold, regardless of whether they had been kings or paupers in their homeland. Itapoan pointed out the difference between the slaves that submitted and "even were admitted inside the white master's house," and others who rebelled and ran away and were punished with an iron necklace with protruding branches that would inhibit and embarrass them if they tried to enter the woods again. Other slaves were forbidden to talk to these recaptured rebels.

He showed Rugendas' "Jogar capüera" drawing (1834), pointing out, "There is no berimbau, just an *atabaque* drum, chanting, and clapping, and it seems there was no *floreio*, kicks, or game on the ground but the *cabeçada* was heavily used." However, in two other Debret drawings from the same period we see the berimbau, called *"urucungo"* but dissociated from the capoeira game. "We don't know how or why the African *'urucungo'* began to be called 'berimbau,' which was the name of a small European musical instrument [jew's-harp or jaw-harp] made of a thin blade of metal played by using the mouth as a resonance box."

Mestre Itapoan also showed drawings of the *"entrudo,"* from which Rio's Carnival would develop, and commented, "Already in those times, as we see in the drawings, the *'entrudo'* created problems with shop owners and rich people. When the poor had fun this was always considered a 'problem'."

He showed drawings from Kalixto (1906) depicting Rio's capoeira gangs fighting each other using the *cabeçada, rasteira,* switchblades, daggers, and wooden clubs. As the historical review reached our time he showed many newspaper articles focusing on Bimba and other mestres from the 1930s and later. He criticized Bahia's tourism institutions, "which used again and again the images of these late mestres without giving them anything in return."

Finally he showed newspaper clips from the 1970s when Bimba, already over 70 years old, became dissatisfied with Salvador's authorities and decided to leave Bahia. He went to Goiania state (near the capital, Brasília), where there were promises that Bimba would be supported. Before leaving Salvador, Bimba said about Goiania: "If I cannot enjoy anything there at least I'll enjoy its cemetery." In fact, less than four years later (1974) Bimba, aged 74, unhappy and partly abandoned, passed away in Goiania.

Mestre Itapoan and other pupils went there and brought his body back to be buried in Salvador. This was considered a sacrilege by many because Bimba had sworn he would never return. In the photos of the seventh-day mass in a Catholic church, we also see Mestre Pastinha, well into his eighties. The antagonism between the two was "in great part created by the press: they visited one another. Pastinha sent Bimba invitations and Bimba had gone to Pastinha's book release [in the 1960s]."

In 1981, it would be Mestre Pastinha's turn to die in miserable circumstances, 92 years old and blind, abandoned by Bahia's authorities and institutions.

Mestre Itapoan told how many good players had left Salvador for Rio and São Paulo, seeking better work conditions from the 1970s on. "This caused the capoeira level to fall and only now [in 1984] is Bahia recouping the lost space with the rebirth of a serious Capoeira Angola linked to its roots."

As far as the Federations were concerned, Itapoan said, "Many have gone through the championship thing, but now most think it has no interest at all." The Boxing and Fighting Federation from Bahia wasn't even able to maintain boxing, so "how could it take care of and help an adoptive daughter such as capoeira?" Itapoan concluded, "I am not interested in sport capoeira, but on the other hand I'm not radically against the Federations. At this moment I want capoeira as *'vadiação'* [having fun without 'serious' goals or compromises]."

Then came the questions and answers.

Mestre Bodinho, from Rio, asked why Itapoan said during his speech that "concerning the uniform, the *angoleiros* [Capoeira Angola players] are closer to the truth."

Mestre Itapoan said, "I think things that are pre-established and predetermined are dangerous. My ideal is similar to Caetano Veloso's song [he is a famous singer also from Bahia]: 'It's forbidden to forbid.' When Mestre João Pequeno wants to play capoeira, he doesn't say, 'Excuse me, I'm going to put on my uniform in the bathroom.' He plays as he is if he wants to."

Mestre Gato, from Rio's Senzala, said, "It's true that in the old days capoeira was more spontaneous, but times have changed. If somebody goes to the academy after school or work, how should he play? With his working clothes or the ones from school? The capoeira uniform is a practical way to solve these situations."

Mestre Itapoan agreed but added, "The obligatory use of a uniform reminds me of when I was a kid in school and could not get in because I was wearing blue socks and the school's uniform was black socks. I find that ridiculous."

Mestre João Pequeno commented, "Capoeira has no uniform. The clothes are used by the capoeiristas and they are the ones who really exist. Capoeira is a form of exercising yourself but it is also a form of fighting. If someone gets hit on the street, he can't ask: 'Wait a minute, I'm going to put my uniform on.' In reality the uniform is a pre-set thing, typical of a school or an academy, but not of capoeira." He said that Mestre Pastinha used a black-and-yellow uniform in his academy, which were the colors of the Ypiranga Soccer Club. "Pastinha was a great fan of the Ypiranga. In my academy I use the same capoeira as his [Pastinha's], but I established another type of uniform that has nothing to do with soccer clubs."

Mestre Sorriso, from Rio's Senzala (and now, in 2002, teaching in the south of France) said, "I give classes at PUC [Rio's expensive Catholic University] and I and my pupils have to wear uniforms or else we have problems with the university." Several teachers from Senzala have given classes at PUC continuously since 1970, and in 1984 capoeira was still seen as something "bizarre" that created "problems," while other martial arts and sports didn't have that stigma at all. Now in 2002 the situation is very much the same, although during these thirty years capoeiristas never created or had any real problems in the university. For this same reason Sorriso had to cut his afro-styled hair and not wear his earrings at PUC. He noted, "I make a living on capoeira. The system works that way and there is nothing we can do about it. The use of a uniform is another of these concessions." [Since then Mestre Sorriso has changed a lot. His long dreadlocks are part of these changes.]

Mestre Camisa asked Mestre Itapoan to more clearly explain his statement that "Camisa distorts capoeira because all his pupils play and do the *ginga* exactly the same way."

Mestre Itapoan answered that he had seen the theater play "Capitães da Areia" and when an actor "jumped into the scene and did the *ginga*, it was obvious that he was Camisa's pupil. In Bahia and in Bimba's school no one does the *ginga* the same way. The *ginga* is the capoeirista's identity, and that's why I think you distort capoeira."

Mestre Camisa then asked what Itapoan thought was necessary to end the antagonism between Capoeira Angola and Regional.

Mestre Itapoan responded, "This antagonism many times destroyed good friendships. Although many people think capoeira is one, this is not enough because this antagonism is a traditional heritage. In all of Brazil capoeira is one, but in Bahia, like it or not, things are different."

Mestre Acordeon explained how this antagonism began and how things are at the present (1984) moment. (His point of view is a bit different from Mestre Itapoan's.) "Bimba came from Capoeira Angola and created Capoeira Regional. He became very famous and was a strong leader, and this inhibited many mestres of his time. In addition, he was not socially polite and had a very difficult personality to deal with if you were not his pupil. It was not easy to establish a good relationship with him. The antagonism between Regional and Angola appeared over the issue of which style was more efficient as a fight. Bimba had a warrior's temper; this was typical of him and it was passed down to his students. The students felt that 'my mestre's enemies are also my enemies.' It was in this context that the antagonism was born and grew and remains until today."

Mestre Acordeon noted that Camisa-Roxa (another very famous pupil of Bimba's and older brother to Camisa) was the first to establish a bridge between Angola and Regional [in the 1960s] and had been a "very positive influence for capoeira." Camisa-Roxa started going to Angola *rodas* and absorbed many influences that made his style richer. Due to that, his relationship with his mestre (Bimba) was damaged. "We see this highly positive influence from Angola today reflected in Camisa's way of playing."

Mestre Acordeon said, "Now there is nobody to represent the same tradition and mentality as our old mestre. The old ideas of 'school,' 'group unity,' and 'antagonism toward angoleiros' don't exist as in the old days." Acordeon said he saw something that would have been impossible while Bimba was alive: there was a party at Bimba's academy (now directed by one of his former pupils) with "many Angoleiros invited, and the first game was an Angola one. Pastinha and Bimba, Angola and Regional—this unity will happen in the future and is already happening because there is no one from the old way of thinking to impede it."

It's true that in the last twenty years there has been more of a bridge between certain Angola and Regional players. But I think this happened mostly among some of the capoeiristas who were reaching 40 years of age. I think some of them were more mature and could relate to someone they admired, notwithstanding he was from a different "tribe."

But among the younger players (and some of the older as well), I saw an exaggerated antagonism, especially in the late 1980s and early 1990s. This was not specifically between *angoleiros* and *regionais* but even between teachers and pupils of the same group. It reached the point where there was some shooting in broad daylight in one of Rio's most famous streets involving two rival academies belonging to the same group. In São Paulo's Praça da Liberdade street *roda* this was also a period of overwhelmingly stupid violence. In the mid 1990s, things calmed down, maybe because the mestres realized that violence was getting out of control and this could be harmful (economically) for everyone if the media focused on what was happening.

This extreme violence and competition is, in my opinion, the result of the ego and personality of mestres of different groups. They develop certain strategies based on competition among their own pupils and antagonism toward other groups that are passed on to their pupils.

While one can criticize strategies that use too much violence, this doesn't mean that competition is all "bad." Deleuze and Guattari, in *Mille Plateaux*, describe certain internal mechanisms in the "nomad structure" (which exists in opposition to the "sedentary structure" that we see in our cities and nation-states) in order to prevent the growth of a "sedentary structure" (such as the Capoeira Confederation) inside a "nomad structure" (such as the many independent capoeira groups which do not acknowledge any central power). The competition and even the antagonism between groups is one of these "mechanisms of prevention." It interferes with the ability of groups to mingle and work together, in order to create such a big complex that rigid rules and laws become necessary to organize the whole thing. (I focus on this issue in another book.) I believe that one of the secrets of capoeira's success and expansion is its "nomad structure." And I hope it will continue that way. Nevertheless, I am totally against violence in the *rodas*—something quite different from a "rough game" done to the proper berimbau rhythm.

Falcão, from Salvador, asked what could be done to ensure that mestres from the *velha guarda* do not go through the same economic difficulties experienced by Pastinha and Bimba.

Mestre Itapoan said, "We have to convince the government that it is their responsibility to take care of these mestres when they reach old age, because they are a true national patrimony. Another suggestion is to contact private industries that may be able to deduct any assistance to the old mestres from their taxes. At any rate, economic help has to be constant, every month, and not just occasional."

Mestre Camisa steered the conversation back to Mestre Acordeon's comment about "the 'distortion' Itapoan sees in my pupils' *ginga*." Camisa agreed that "the *ginga* is something personal," but as capoeira is also a fighting form, "the fact is that some body positions are better than others." Mestre Camisa explained that his method is "to relate attack and defense positions to an axis." For example, he doesn't let his pupils stretch out their front leg during the *ginga* "because if they receive a *pisão* on the stretched knee they would be seriously injured." Similarly, he said that he advised pupils against crossing the back leg (the feet should move as if on a triangle), because they could be vulnerable to a *banda*."

Mestre Camisa continued, "I tell my pupils not to support themselves with only their fingers on the ground; the whole hand should be on the ground. The position of the arms in order to protect, attack, or maintain balance is critical, and each blow and movement has its own position. Everything evolves and there has to be study on any subject." He himself has been observing and studying capoeira for a long time. "Even when you play to have fun you must be watchful and cautious. There are many players with good potential but their 'house' is not properly organized. Today there are more players at a high level, and this is due to the studies and teaching methods recently developed." He concluded by saying, "Notwithstanding all this, if I were to play a capoeira *malandreada* [full of *malícia*] with a good *angoleiro*, I'm not going to do a robot *ginga* in front of him.... But one must have specific positions for the *ginga*."

Many capoeira players search for a "scientific basis" to their teaching method. The *ginga* must be "a perfect triangle," and so forth. They don't seem to understand that "simple science"—arithmetic, geometry, etc.—can solve "simple" problems but cannot be applied to "complex systems" because its scope is limited.

Nevertheless, many teachers believe that their system is "scientific" and therefore more "legitimate." The "scientific method and approach" makes them "better" than other groups that are still linked to the "old ways." If one of our "scientific" capoeiristas could have a small glimpse of what today's advanced science actually is, he might be surprised how it often converges with traditional knowledge of ancient civilizations.

Then Mestre Garrincha asked Mestre Itapoan how he passed on to his pupils the "*vadiação* spirit" he talked about toward the end of his speech.

Mestre Itapoan answered that in reality "to play capoeira is to *vadiar* [to do nothing, 'to bum around and not work'], to play for pleasure and for fun with no preconceived objectives or goals." When a teacher takes a pupil to the *roda,* "he is taking that beginner to the *'vadiação'.*" Itapoan then gave an anecdote about Mestre Valdemar, from Salvador's "old guard," who once said to a younger player that tried to grab him (while developing what the younger player thought to be "an objective way of playing"): "Please don't touch me, don't grab me, don't mess up my clothes. When I leave the *roda* the only tidying up I pretend to do is to wash my hands." In Valdemar's ironic remark we clearly see "the difference between someone who plays with a *'vadiação* mood' and one who plays with a competitive edge."

Mestre Gato Preto, from Salvador (don't mistake him for the much younger Gato from Rio's Senzala), commented, "Capoeira was born as a defense and necessity of the men who had no weapons—the negroes. It evolved, and from one it passed on to a million negroes. I'm black but I hold no racism against whites. Nevertheless, some things must be explained. Mestre Bimba, originally an *angoleiro,* created Regional. With time a group of white students surrounded him and in a certain way they even had the power to command things. Although Bimba was an exceptional man, he was ignorant. And the truth is that blacks had little opportunity to attend Bimba's academy and learn Regional. I'm not saying there were no blacks in Regional," continued Gato Preto, "but for each six hundred whites there were only six blacks, while in Angola 80% were black. Many young negroes become lawless because they don't have proper guidance or the opportunities that whites have. I would like to see the blacks participating [in the leadership of the capoeira movement] together with you [the white majority of the 30- to 40-year-old generation that was leading capoeira in 1984]. I want union. This antagonism must end or it'll continue until the days of my great-grandson."

Mestre Moraes, an Afro-Brazilian of the same age group (in 1984) as the leading Regional-Senzala generation, trained with Pastinha in Salvador. He commented on several issues that were on that night's agenda, including distortions and loss of roots in capoeira.

"As Mestre Gato Preto said, while an elite majority started to absorb capoeira, the black man lost space, and distortions were introduced. Capoeira Angola was even called 'capoeira for girls,' and the newly arrived [white middle-class players] wanted to impose a style of capoeira that they thought was 'a capoeira meant for killing.' It is getting difficult to preserve capoeira. New bad mestres are graduated by older bad mestres," pronounced Moraes, "and these new academies get filled up with pupils that are going to be bad players."

Mestre Moraes looked around and added, "Whoever find that their head fits the hat [his criticisms] might use it." He continued, "If today's players really worried about maintaining capoeira's tradition, there would be no need for us to be here, in this room, talking about it: we would be playing. However, here we are trying to mend something that has been wrong for a long, long time, and I say that this sort of thing cannot be mended and that is why normally I don't come to this sort of event. Some Regional players used to say, 'We put the *angoleiros* on the ground and step on their heads.' But I come from Salvador and I teach Angola, and I demand that my work be respected. If that isn't possible by exchanging ideas then we are going to play capoeira and see how things go."

Mestre Moraes also commented on the use of judo and karate in capoeira, another distortion of the game. He criticized people who sung Gilberto Gil's and Martinho da Villa's [two famous composers/singers of Brazilian music] songs in the capoeira *roda* as "capoeiristas who don't know what capoeira music is." He said, "The *roda* must have three berimbaus, the *gunga* [deep-toned], *médio* [medium], and *violinha* [high-pitched], each in its proper and specific function, as well as the *pandeiro,* and the *atabaque* and *agogo* could also be part of the ensemble." He stressed that mothers should watch out where they put their children to learn capoeira so they do not become "one of these gladiators that we so often see." He said that the number of players who left Brazil to go abroad "is proportional to the support they find abroad. What holds me back in Brazil [Moraes had been invited to deliver a workshop in the US] are my pupils who love Capoeira Angola."

He concluded by saying, "They called Pastinha 'the king of Capoeira Angola' but Pastinha didn't have any chance to face the lack of character of those who gave him a *rasteira* when he had, metaphorically speaking, only one leg to stand on."

RACISM IN CAPOEIRA

The discussion around capoeira in Bahia inevitably shifted to racism, a topic rarely broached in public settings. It evolved to include racism in other places and within Senzala. Earlier, Lua had asked pointedly, "Why isn't Garrincha part of the committee that organized this meeting?" (Garrincha and Nagô were the only two black "red-ropes" in Senzala in 1984; the other fourteen were white.)

Mestre Garrincha addressed this later, saying that he started learning capoeira as a kid, and "with time I became conscious that I was the only black 'red-rope' in Senzala for more than ten years." He asked himself, 'What should I do? Leave the group because I'm black? Turn my back on those who introduced me to capoeira?' He commented that another black, Sorriso, who grew up with him and also entered Senzala as a kid, had not yet received his red-rope. But this was not due to the color of his skin but because Sorriso stopped capoeira for three years and then started to train again. Garrincha noted that Bimba, a black man, was Senzala's main reference, and that cut out any possibility of racism. "Senzala exists. When I ask support from its other members I receive it. Lua thinks I ought to teach capoeira in the *favela* [ghetto, slums]. But I teach at PUC [a private university]. It's there that I develop my work. I've had problems with racism, including with some of my white pupils. But I managed to bypass these problems by bringing the other person closer to me. And regardless of that, I have no prejudice against anyone."

Mestre Miguel, an Afro-Brazilian from Bahia who was then

teaching in the south of Brazil, said, "Capoeira encompasses social, political, historic and racial issues, and it is important to stress that racism exists at different levels. There is a paternalistic relation [from the whites toward the black teachers], a relation of submission inside the Senzala Group that I do not like to acknowledge."

Mestre Gato, one of Senzala's founders, then asked Mestre Miguel, "When did you or Garrincha or Sorriso [black Senzala teachers] ever suffer discrimination inside Senzala?"

Mestre Miguel answered, "It was obvious due to the general attitude, the distance toward the black capoeirista." He said that several times he had been criticized by Camisa and Caio (both from Senzala at that time) because he was teaching only blacks (in São Paulo). "Capoeira does not exist without black men," he added.

Gato said to Miguel, "You might have perceived a paternalistic attitude toward Garrincha and Sorriso because they came into the group as kids [about eight or nine years old]. Sometimes they might be treated as younger brothers but always as brothers." Gato went on to explain that there were few blacks in Senzala due to a socioeconomic problem: the academy charged a fee to its students in order to survive, and the middle-class students who had their fees paid by a father were mostly white. (The majority of students in 1984 were teenagers or youngsters who lived with their parents.) Most blacks don't have this opportunity. When they are 18 or younger, they already have to work, and only the very exceptional manage to do a capoeira class after hard work from seven to five. It would be great to develop these kids in the *favela,* but the capoeira teacher would have to be paid by the government or by some other institution, Mestre Gato concluded.

The fact is that many capoeira players, including some of Gato's Senzala colleagues, gave capoeira classes in *favelas,* charging only a symbolic fee. (Capoeiristas say you should never give something entirely for free because people don't value it.) In Copacabana, in the *favela* up Sacopã Street, Eugenio "Boquinha" gave classes for a couple of years starting in the late 1960s, and then Lua "Rasta,"

Flavio "Visual," "Visorama," and I (Nestor) took up this task.

It's rewarding to take capoeira to the *favelas* because people there don't have the money to pay a normal academy's fee. Furthermore, many don't feel comfortable going to an established academy and asking for a scholarship, which many times is given to the new pupil who shows that he is dedicating himself to capoeira. But it's more interesting if you also have an academy "down in the streets" where you can install the pupils who really are giving it an honest try.

Most people who live in a *favela* look for chances to enlarge their social circles and usual context. People who don't live in the *favela* might romanticize parts of that life, but in fact, it is very uncomfortable to live in a shack knowing that at any moment someone might kick the door down, including police or the local drug dealers. And if you shoot one of these mothers, believe me, you are going to have problems.

Mestre Miguel then said that Camisa once commented that there were twenty blacks doing kung-fu in the same academy where he taught capoeira for the same price, meaning that those blacks preferred to do an exotic martial art that was "in fashion" due to current kung-fu movies than to engage in capoeira, which belongs to black Brazilian culture. "But we must have in mind that a sociopolitical apparatus exists in order to separate the negroes from their culture," said Mestre Miguel. "Racial discrimination exists not only inside Senzala but in general. In São Paulo I repeatedly see discrimination against negroes inside capoeira academies, ridiculed with comments and jokes such as 'Man! look at that thick lip hanging from his mouth'."

Mestre Miguel concluded, "This meeting has a positive overall balance because different opinions have been presented and antagonistic points of view had equal chance to express themselves."

I will take this opportunity to comment on the absurdity of racial discrimination and prejudice inside the capoeira world. This issue had seldom been discussed publicly before our 1984 meeting.

Racism exists in all of Brazil. It is different from what we find in the US, but it is definitely present.

Everyone knows this, although many (mostly whites who want a "politically correct" image of Brazil) say there is no racial discrimination in Brazil, that what exists is economic discrimination.

Gilberto Gil (one of Brazil's most famous singers) once said in an interview that one of Salvador's elite clubs was forbidden to blacks, and thus Gil had to enter through a back door. And this happened in Salvador, where we know that racial mixture is everywhere, in all families at all economic levels.

Racial prejudice exists everywhere, and that includes capoeira.

Some mestres do, in fact, have more of an "economic discrimination" in their academies. They don't want poor people in it, even if they are white, but especially not if they are black. This sort of mestre generally is struggling to enter the upper middle class. They may be called "mestres," but in my opinion they are a mediocre bunch.

But there is an even worse group of teachers and mestres and players.

These are racists who discriminate against people purely on the basis of the color of their skin. Luckily, this is a smaller group.

Some of them are openly racist, which is not as common in Brazil as it is in some parts of America. They don't like blacks and consider them "inferior." Paradoxically, these same guys consider themselves "capoeiristas," a culture that was born and to a great extent developed in the black cultural arena.

Others may have skin color prejudice but don't admit it or show it openly. Instead they show their true feelings by the jokes and comments they make. We find this sort of person everywhere.

In the Senzala group this spectrum of racism also exists, at least in my opinion and based on my experience in the group.

One of my "red-rope" colleagues is widely known as a racist, and he not only admits it but is proud of it. He is always making deprecating jokes about dark-skinned people. He also discriminates against everybody who does not live in the rich southern zone of Rio. All of this causes embarrassment to many of the other "red-ropes," regardless of where they stand on the racism issue. In fact, this overtly racist colleague started to be discriminated against by most of the other "red-ropes." He is seldom invited to perform in shows or to participate in different events.

There are three or four others who have a strong racial prejudice as well as a social and economic one, but they disguise it. Maybe they don't even accept the racist label. Notwithstanding their prejudice, some have black friends, all accept black pupils, and they even give scholarships to beginners, white or black, who don't have money but dedicate themselves to training and show strong potential.

I think the majority of "red-ropes" at the time of this conference (1984) were people who don't have racial prejudice. That is, if it is possible for someone who lives in a discriminating society to be "absolutely non-discriminative." Maybe this proportion—one racist, four disguised racists, and ten non-racists—could apply to a great portion of the capoeira context.

I should also point out that there is an inverse kind of racism of blacks against whites and even of blacks against mulattos. This kind of discrimination became more apparent after the social wave that valorized Afro-Americans in the United States (Malcolm X, "black is beautiful," etc.). And this is understandable. Brazil is, to a large extent, an economic and cultural colony of the US, and everything that happens in the States has repercussions in Brazil.

But it is also true that although the entire black population feels deeply the sting and weight of discrimination, only a minority of them (compared to the percentage of white racists) have a radical prejudice against whites in general or against whites in the capoeira world.

This issue of "racism inside capoeira" might seem strange to an outsider, especially given that capoeira was born in the black community and largely evolved there. But it is only strange for those who do not deeply know Bahia, Rio, and Recife—the three centers where capoeira developed since the eighteenth and nineteenth centuries.

In these three centers we find racism firmly implanted for centuries. Despite its repulsive character, it shows itself in such ridiculous ways that one might almost laugh if it weren't so sad: "whites" who belong to families that have many blacks in their past (the majority of Brazilian families) posing as "completely white" and showing racial prejudice against blacks and light-skinned mulattos; light-skinned mulattos discriminating against "blacks"; dark-skinned blacks with whites in their family history posing as "pure blacks" and discriminating against whites, mulattos, light-skinned people, etc.

The truth is it is difficult to find people with a wide vision of life, regardless of their social class, religion, sex, and skin color.

TALKS WITH THE VELHA GUARDA

Back to the 1984 conference. The talk with the mestres of the *"velha guarda"* was more informal than the speeches of the meeting's previous days. Groups of capoeiristas gathered around the mestres, asking them questions, hearing what they had to tell. It was a good idea that worked well, but unfortunately I could not be at different places at the same time, so most of what was discussed was not recorded.

Nevertheless I interviewed Mestres Valdemar, João Grande, Canjiquinha, and Atenilo about an interesting issue. We had all seen the presentations of groups from eight different states as well as six groups from Rio, so I asked the old mestres what they thought of contemporary capoeira (1984) compared to the capoeira practiced when they were young (circa the 1940s).

I must repeat that almost all groups presenting themselves were from Senzala or strongly influenced by the Regional-Senzala style of playing. Martin's and Corvo's groups from the outskirts of Rio were a bit less susceptible to Senzala, since their major influence was Mestre Artur Emidio, who had come from Itabuna (in Bahia) in the 1950s. The only real exception was Moraes' Angola group, Pelourinho.

It was around 1985 (a year or so after the conference) that Angola style started to become popular again to the point that today (2002) maybe 30% of capoeira is strongly influenced by the Angola style or claims to be "legitimate Angola." So we must understand that the old mestres' comments about "contemporary capoeira" in 1984 are mostly directed toward the Senzala style that was hegemonic in the capoeira world from approximately 1970 to 1990. Even today its influence is obvious in at least 60% of the capoeira played internationally.

I talked to each mestre individually, and their responses had a common point: they liked and even were impressed with contemporary capoeira, and there was not a general feeling of "loss of roots and distortion."

In that sense, they were quite different from our contemporary "prophets of the Apocalypse," who use their radical criticism and speeches as a strategy to disparage other groups while themselves trying to gain more power, more students, and more influence in the capoeira world.

The old mestres, as we have seen, showed themselves to be quite flexible and open toward new developments such as women in capoeira, but they were strongly opposed to other things such as the creation of a "world" capoeira association outside Brazil.

In regard to the game itself, the old mestres thought that something had been gained (especially in the strength and speed of the kicks), and something had been lost in capoeira (slyness, smartness, *malícia*).

Mestre Canjiquinha started capoeira in 1936.

"I'm old but I'm not going to obscure the truth," he said. "Capoeira now is better in several ways."

He said that in his days the most feared blows were the *cabeçada* (head-butt) and *rasteira* (swiping with the foot to trip someone). "The blows with the feet [*meia-lua, armada, queixada,* etc.] were slow, not very powerful, and not very dangerous except when delivered at the exact moment when the face of the other guy was totally vulnerable. They didn't have the strength and the speed of today's kicks. Today's *queixada,* for example, can kill someone."

Canjiquinha concluded by saying that if he were young he would be "training with the rest of the gang and developing this part. But it's also true that today's players have lost a lot in regard to *malícia* and the '*visão de jogo*' [vision of the game, being able to see and understand what is going on and to set up traps]."

Mestre João Pequeno, 66 years old in 1984, amazed everyone by playing more than ten times in one of the evening *rodas.* He thinks capoeira in Salvador, Rio, and São Paulo is at the same level, but in Rio and São Paulo it has more "mass development" (more players, more high-level students, but everyone playing with a similar style).

He thinks capoeira gained a lot in the kicks and in the "artistic" part (fascinating the public by its rapid and acrobatic movements). "But it lost in the '*brincadeira*' aspect [playing for fun] and the '*fundamento da malícia*' [to have *malícia* while playing]," said João Pequeno. "It also lost in spontaneity. The blows are good but the sequence of blows, one after the other, looks like something rehearsed."

Mestre João Pequeno continued, "Capoeira needs to have three basic things: one, for the public to watch (this is the 'artistic part,' which is well developed today); two, the 'inside capoeira' part must be present (something that reflects the soul of the player); and third is the part that is done in the moment (improvisation, creativity, spontaneous movements that have not been trained in classes). Today's capoeira has lost a lot from the two last parts."

It has also lost in endurance, he added. "The games are short, less than three minutes, while in my time it was common for a game to go on for fifteen minutes. Maybe this is due to the effort of giving very fast blows, one after the other, but it is also due to not being relaxed and not having a proper dynamic of movement during the game."

Later, as I talked with Mestres Canjiquinha and João Pequeno at the same time, they agreed that "the development of faster and more powerful kicks is no doubt the result of the teaching method where you systematically repeat the same blow dozens of times with all the students doing the *ginga* and performing the blows together, following the teacher's lead."

In their days, the game itself was trained, as two players freely played with each other. That didn't methodically develop the technique of each blow, but on the other hand, it developed the game itself, the "vision of the game" (the ability to see what is going on at each moment and almost to know what is coming next), and the *"malícia."*

The old masters also commented that many newer players use only four or five blows and a couple of movements. "They don't have the resources to move freely (instead they all use 'clichés' for moving around) nor the capacity to fool the opponent. The game is essentially an exchange of those few blows at high speed."

They again noted that different types of *cabeçada* (head-butt) were once used in both the standing position and in the game near the floor. They were extremely dangerous and violent. Today's players have "lost the art of *cabeçada,* substituting the kicks for it."

Mestre João Pequeno said that he had changed his teaching method. Previously he "taught the students one by one, and the rest watched. The pupil trained less in each class but he watched more." By 1984 he had incorporated "a warm-up with all students using Capoeira Angola movements." He changed the training of the different blows such that students stand in line, approach one by one, give a certain blow, and retreat using the *rolê* or some other movement, returning to the end of the line.

This method was also very common in Rio when I started in the 1960s. My first mestre, Leopoldina, used it.

When I went to Senzala around 1968, I experienced their new (at that time) method of everybody doing the *ginga* together, following the teacher's movement in front of the class, and repeating each blow ten or twenty times. We also trained in doubles, repeat-

215

THE LITTLE CAPOEIRA BOOK

ing the same blow dozens of times with the outstretched hand of a partner as a target. (These two techniques were adapted from karate, which was very popular in Rio at the time due to the arrival from Japan of a high-level black-belt Shotokan *sensei* called Tanaka.) Bimba's sequence was another training format. With time, many teachers started developing and using their own sequences.

Mestre João Pequeno says he is searching for an intermediary method between the "traditional method" and the "mass method" of modern times. He says he is satisfied with the results.

Then I talked with Mestre Atenilo, the only one of the old mestres who represented Capoeira Regional. He trained with Bimba while Bimba still taught Angola style—prior to his creating Regional.

"As far as the kicks are concerned, modern capoeira is spectacular," he said, "but it lost in the realm of tricks and smartness." In Atenilo's opinion the contemporary player doesn't know how to set up a trap. The attacks and defenses today are good, but lost are the *cabeçada,* the technique of *"trancar"* ("to lock" the opponent's game, not letting the other develop his movement strategy), and the art of *"amarrar"* ("to tie up" the other's movements, not giving space to the other). It is important to point out that *"amarrar"* and *"trancar"* do not mean grabbing or bumping and trying to crudely run over the opponent by force. They are sophisticated resources used by those who develop *"visão de jogo"* (vision of the game), and many times the technique requires putting yourself in the right place, in the proper position, for that specific moment.

"The *rasteira* is no longer widely used," noted Mestre Atenilo, "although it is a very valuable weapon, especially when you are attacked in a small space and cannot deliver a round blow such as the *meia-lua-de-compasso* or *queixada.*"

Mestre Atenilo concluded that many of these features are lacking as the result of playing far away from one another. "It seems the players are afraid of each other. You need to *'unir'* ['unite,' stay close to your opponent], to play more *dentro* [inside, or closer], to avoid giving so many blows *fora* [outward] that will not hit the opponent because you are not close enough or because your timing wasn't good." Atenilo concluded that "giving your blows *fora* means that the opponent doesn't even have to dodge them and can give another blow *fora* at very high speed." But being so far apart, "it is difficult to give a *cabeçada,* a *rasteira,* or to go in and take the guy down." In his opinion it is necessary "to play *dentro* to better develop the guard and the *'entrar'* [going in] because it's from the *união* [union] that is born the *'malícia do barulho'* [the slyness and smartness of the troublemaking]," he concluded with a laugh.

In general, the old masters commented on other issues relative to distortion and disrespect for the ritual of the game, including:

- starting the game before the singer has finished singing the *ladainha* (litany, starting song);

- students that *comprar* (buy) a game when a mestre is playing;

- players that *"comprar"* the game, not letting the previous game develop itself, etc.

But they didn't think that these were "basic" distortions that "disabled contemporary capoeira."

The distortions were a secondary thing that in their opinion could be easily changed with each mestre teaching the proper procedures to his or her pupils. In their way of seeing things, the old mestres considered these "distortions" and "lack of roots" to be something "external." The real dangers of distortion reside in "internal" factors, such as how the minds of these young, contemporary mestres and players function in an overwhelming society of technology, mass culture, military values, television, propaganda, consumerism, and stereotyped, spoon-fed, and mediocre values. Indeed, with these powerful global influences, one wonders how anything "traditional," anything with roots, will fare in the twenty-first century.

A final note: Since 1984, Mestres Canjiquinha, Atenilo, Gato Preto, Paulo dos Anjos, Ezequiel, and many other dear friends have passed away.

We miss them.

We feel their presence in every *roda*.

BIBLIOGRAPHY

ABREU, Frederico J. de. *Bimba é bamba, a capoeira no ringue.* Salvador: Instituto Jair Moura, 1999.

ALMEIDA, M.A. *Memórias de um sargento de milícia.* Rio de Janeiro: INL, 1944.

ALMEIDA, R.C.A (Mestre Itapoã). *Bimba, perfil do* mestre. Salvador: Centro Editorial e Didático da UFBA, 1982.

_____. *Mestre 'Atenilo,' o relâmpago da capoeira regional.* Salvador: Núcleo de Recursos Didáticos da UFBa, 1988.

_____. *Bibliografia crítica da capoeira.* Brasília: DEFER, CIDOCA/DF, 1993.

ALMEIDA, Ubirajara de (Mestre Acordeon). *Capoeira, A Brazilian Art Form.* Berkeley, CA, USA: North Atlantic Books, 1986.

_____. *Agua de beber, camará!* Salvador: EGBA, 1999.

AMADO, G. *Minha formação no Recife.* Rio de Janeiro, 1955.

AMADO, J. *Bahia de todos os santos.*

ANTONIO, João. *Leão de chácara.* Rio de Janeiro: Civilização Brasileira, 1976.

AREIAS, Almir das. *O que é capoeira.* São Paulo: Braziliense, 1983.

ASSIS, M. *Crônicas.* Rio de Janeiro: W.M. Jackson Inc.

AZEVEDO, A. *O cortiço.* São Paulo: Martins Fontes, 1965.

BARBIERI, Cesar. *Um jeito Brazileiro de aprender a ser.* Brasília: DEFER CIDOCA/DF, 1993.

BARRETO FILHO, Melo, and LIMA, Hermeto. *História da polícia do Rio de Janeiro 1565–1831.* Rio de Janeiro: Ed. S.A. A Noite, 1939.

BIMBA, Mestre. *Curso de capoeira regional.* Salvador: s/ed., s/data.

BRETAS, M.L. "Navalhas e capoeiras," *Ciência Hoje* v.10 n.59. Rio de Janeiro: SBPC, 1989.

BURLAMAQUI, A. *Gymnastica Nacional (capoeiragem) Methodizada e Regrada.* Rio de Janeiro: /s.n./, 1928.

CAPOEIRA, N. *O pequeno manual do jogador de capoeira.* São Paulo: Ground, 1981.

_____. *Galo já cantou.* Rio de Janeiro: ArteHoje, 1985.

_____. *Capoeira, os fundamentos da malícia.* Rio de Janeiro: Record, 1992.

_____. *Capoeira, le petit manuel du jouer.* Paris: ATABAC, 1995.

_____. *The Little Capoeira Book.* Berkeley, CA: North Atlantic Books, 1995.

_____. *A balada de Noivo-da-Vida e Veneno-da-Madrugada.* Rio de Janeiro: Record, 1997.

_____. and BORGHALL, J. *Capoeira, kampdans og livsfilosofi fra Brazilien.* Odense, Denmark: Odense University, 1997.

_____. "Manduca da Praia, violência, poder, dinheiro, e valentia." *Revista Capoeira nº3.* São Paulo, set./out. 1998.

_____. *Capoeira, galo já cantou.* Rio de Janeiro: Record, 1999.

_____. *Capoeira, Kampfkunst und Tanz aus Brazilien.* Berlin: Weinmann, 1999.

_____. *Capoeira, pequeno manual do jogador de capoeira.* Rio de Janeiro: Record, 1999.

CARNEIRO, Edison. *Capoeira, cadernos de folclore n.14.* Rio de Janeiro: 1971.

_____. *Negros Bantus: notas de ethonographia religiosa e de folk-lore.* Rio de Janeiro: Civilização Brazileira, 1937.

CASCUDO, Camara. *Folclore do Brazil.* Rio de Janeiro: Fundo de Cultura Brazil-Portugal, 1967.

COELHO NETO, H.M. *Bazar.* Rio de Janeiro: Zelio Valverde, 1942.

COSTA, L.P. *Capoeira sem mestre.* Rio de Janeiro: Tecnoprint, /s.d.

D'ANUNCIAÇÃO, L. *Berimbau, a percussão dos ritmos Brazileiros, v.1.* Rio de Janeiro: Europa, 1990.

DEBRET. *Voyage pittoresque et historique au Brésil.* Paris: Didot

Firmin et Fréres, 1834.

DECANIO FILHO, Angelo A. (Mestre Decanio). *Falando em capoeira*. Salvador: Col. São Salomão, 1996. Photoc.

_____. *Herança da mestre Bimba, lógica e filosofia africanas da capoeira*. Salvador: Col. São Salomão, 1996. Photoc.

_____. *A herança de Pastinha*. Salvador: Col. São Salomão n°3, 1996.

DELEUZE, G., and GUATTARI, F. *Mille plateaux*. Paris: Les Editions de Minuit, 1980.

DURST, Rogério. *Madame Satã*. São Paulo: Braziliense, 1985.

EDMUNDO, L. *O Rio de Janeiro do meu tempo, vol II*. Rio de Janeiro: Conquista, 1957.

HOBSBAWN, Eric J. *Era dos extremos, o breve sec.XX, 1914–1991*. São Paulo: Cia. das Letras, 1995.

HOBSBAWN, Eric, e RANGER, T. *A invenção das tradições*. Rio de Janeiro: Paz e Terra, 1984.

HOLLOWAY, T. *O saudável terror*. Rio de Janeiro: Cadernos Candido Mendes n.16, Estudos Afro-Brazileiros, 1989.

LEMLE, Marina. *A capoeira nas voltas do mundo: na roda, o grupo Senzala*. Rio de Janeiro: Monografia, Jornalismo, Fac. Helio Alonso, 1993.

LEWIS, J.L. *Ring of Liberation*. Chicago: Univ. of Chicago Press, 1992.

LOPES, André L.L. *A volta do mundo da capoeira*. Rio de Janeiro: Coregráfica Editora e Gráfica, 1999.

MARINHO, I.P. *Subsídios para o estudo da metodologia do treinamento da capoeiragem*. Rio de Janeiro: Imprensa Nacional, 1945.

MATTOS, Claudia. *Acertei no milhar*. Rio de Janeiro: Paz e Terra, 1982.

MORAES FILHO, A.J.M. "Capoeiragem e capoeiras célebres," *Festas e tradições populares do Brazil*. Rio de Janeiro: 1901.

MOURA, Jair (Mestre Jair). *Capoeira, a luta regional baiana*. Salvador: Cadernos de Cultura, Prefeitura Municipal de Salvador, 1979.

_____. *Capoeiragem, arte e malandragem*. Salvador: Cadernos de

Cultura nº 2, Pref. Mun. de Salvador, 1980.

_____. "Evolução, apogeu e declínio da capoeiragem no Rio de Janeiro," *Cadernos Rioarte Ano I nº3.* Rio de Janeiro: 1985.

_____. *Mestre Bimba, a crônica da capoeiragem.* Salvador: Fundação Mestre Bimba, 1991.

_____. "A projeção do negro Ciríaco no âmbito da capoeiragem," *Revista Capoeira.* São Paulo: #11, Dec. 1999.

_____. "Um titã da capoeiragem, Plácido de Abreu," *Revista Capoeira.* São Paulo: Ed. Candeia, ano II, #12, Jan. 2001.

MOURA, Roberto. *Tia Ciata e a Pequena África no Rio.* Rio de Janeiro: Col. Biblioteca Carioca, 1995.

ORTIZ, Fernando. *Los instrumentos de la musica afro-cubana, vol.V.* Habana: Cardenas y cia., 1955.

PAEZZO, S. *Memórias de Madame Satã.* Rio de Janeiro: Lidador, 1972.

PASSOS NETO, N.S. *Ritual roda, mandinga x tele-real.* Rio de Janeiro: Dissertação de mestrado, Escola de Comunicação da UFRJ, 1996.

_____. *Jogo e comunicultura.* Rio de Janeiro: Tese de doutorado-rado, Escola de Comunicação da UFRJ, 2001.

PASTINHA, V.F. (Mestre Pastinha). *Caderno e álbum do centro esportivo de capoeira angola.* Salvador: cad. manuscrito, s/date, approx. 1955.

_____. *Capoeira Angola.* Salvador: /s.n./1964.

QUERINO, M.R. A capoeira, *Bahia de outrora.* Salvador: Ed. Progresso, 1955.

REGO, W. *Capoeira Angola,* Salvador: Ed. Itapoan, 1968.

REIS, Leticia V.S. *O mundo de pernas para o ar.* São Paulo: Publisher Brazil, 1997.

RUGENDAS, J.M. *Voyage pittoresque et historique dans le Brésil.* Paris: Engelmann et Cie, 1824.

SALVATORE, M.A.B. *Capoeiras e malandros.* Campinas, SP: Mestrado em História, Unicamp, 1990.

SANTOS, Edras M. (Mestre Damião). *Conversando sobre capoeira.* São José dos Campos: 1996. Photoc.

SILVA, J.M. Pereira da. *Segundo período do reinado de D. Pedro I no Brazil.* Rio de Janeiro: B.L. Garnier, 1871.

SILVA, O.M.T. *Bahia, imagens da terra e do povo.* Salvador: 1951.

SOARES, C.E.L. *A negregada instituição, os capoeiras no Rio de Janeiro.* Rio de Janeiro: Coleção Biblioteca Carioca, Prefeitura do Rio de Janeiro, 1994.

_____. *A capoeira escrava e outras tradições rebeldes no Rio de Janeiro (1808–1850).* Campinas: Ed. da Unicamp-CPHSC, 2001.

SODRÉ, Muniz. *O monopólio da fala.* Rio de Janeiro: Vozes, 1977.

_____. *O social irradiado.* São Paulo: Cortez, 1992.

_____. *Claros e escuros, identidade, povo e mídia no Brazil.* Petrópolis, RJ: Vozes, 1999.

SOUZA, A.N. *Da minha Africa e do Brazil que eu vi.* Angola: Ed. Luanda, s/d.

TAVARES, J.C.S. *Dança de guerra, arquivo-arma.* Rio de Janeiro: Mestrado em Sociologia, UnB, 1984.

VIEIRA, L.R. *Da vadiação a capoeira regional.* Brasília: Dissertação de mestrado, UNB, Jan. 1990.

ZAGURI, José ("Zeca Macapá"). *Da capoeiragem carioca à capoeira regional baiana: uma simbiose comunicativa.* Rio de Janeiro: Monografia, Sociologia e Política, PUC, Dec. 1992.

WINNICOTT, D.W. *O Brincar e a Realidade.* Rio de Janeiro: Imago, 1975.

ABOUT THE AUTHOR

Nestor Capoeira was introduced to the game by Mestre Leopoldina, a living legend in Rio de Janeiro's capoeira scene. Later he
joined the famous *Grupo Senzala* and received his *corda-vermelha*
("red-rope," Senzala's highest graduation) in 1969. For four decades
he has played, studied, presented, and taught capoeira in different
countries.

He was the pioneer of taking capoeira abroad from its birth-
place in Brazil, living and teaching in Europe for ten years in four
different stays, beginning with teaching at The London School of
Contemporary Dance (1971).

He played the main role, a capoeira hero, in *Cordão de Ouro*
(Embrafilme, 1978), the only film on capoeira made in Brazil.

Nestor organized and performed in two one-hour nationwide
Brazilian TV specials on capoeira (TVE, 1979 and '84).

He has produced two CDs (1985, '90) with capoeira and percussion music. He also wrote three books on the subject and an
adventure romance with capoeira heroes, published by a top Brazilian publisher (Record). His books have been translated and published in the USA, France, Denmark, Germany, and Holland.

Nestor has performed with different groups, including his own, in
Brazil and abroad: Sala Cecília Meireles (*Senazala Okê*, Rio, 1968),
Teatro Municipal do Rio, and Teatro Castro Alves (*Ballet Brazileiro
da Bahia*, Rio and Salvador, 1969). Sadler's Wells (*Koanga*, London,
1972). Paradiso and Milkyway (Amsterdam, 1974). Centre Cul-
turelle du Marais (Paris, 1980). Teatro Ipanema (*Galo Já Cantou*,

Rio, 1985). Spejlteltet (Copenhagen, 1995), Expo 2000 (Hanover, 2000), Fabrik (Hamburg, 2001), etc.

Nestor has a master's degree in Communication and Culture (UFRJ, Federal University of Rio de Janeiro, 1995), specializing in the influence of TV on Brazil's popular culture and specifically capoeira. He earned a Ph.D. in 2001 at the same university, focusing on "the expansion of capoeira beyond Brazil in the globalization era."

He gives daily classes at Rio's Planetário da Gávea and spends four to five months abroad giving workshops and participating in capoeira performances and events.